CULTURES OF THE WORLD
Kuwait

Maria O' Shea and Michael Spilling

mc **Marshall Cavendish**
Benchmark
New York

PICTURE CREDITS
Cover: © Tim Graham/Alamy
alttype/reuters/Shannon Stapleton: 34 • Audrius Tomonis: 135 • Bjorn Klingwall: 41, 63, 66, 113, 126 • Essam al-Sudani/AFP/Getty Images: 64 • Helene Rogers/Art Directors: 6, 55, 78, 116 • Hutchison Library: 7,44, 48, 65, 99 • Ian Waldie/Getty Images: 51, 106 • Joe Raedle/Getty Images: 40, 112, 119, 123 • Mark Daffey/Getty Images: 2, 9, 56 • Mark Daffey/Lonely Planet Images:1, 5, 8, 52, 53, 60, 72, 86, 104 • Philippe Desmazes/AFP/Getty Images: 47 • photolibrary: 14, 16,17, 18, 29, 54, 59, 62, 90, 130, 131 • Seyllou/AFP/Getty Images: 38 • Thomas Hartwell/Time Life Pictures/Getty Images: 25 • Tim Graham/Getty Images: 68, 118 • Time Life Pictures/Getty Images: 26 • Topham Picturepoint: 24, 36, 77, 81, 88, 114 • Trip Photographic Library:10, 12, 30, 49, 50, 69, 71, 76, 79, 82, 83, 85, 87, 89, 92, 93, 97, 101, 103, 105, 115, 117, 128 • Yasser al-Zayyat/AFP/Getty Images: 28, 31, 33, 37, 67, 73, 75, 94, 95, 108, 120, 121, 124

PRECEDING PAGE
Two Kuwaiti girls smile for the camera.

Publisher (U.S.): Michelle Bisson
Editors: Deborah Grahame, Stephanie Pee
Copyreader: Sherry Chiger
Designer: Bernard Go Kwang Meng
Cover picture researcher: Connie Gardner
Picture researcher: Thomas Khoo

Marshall Cavendish Benchmark
99 White Plains Road
Tarrytown, NY 10591
Web site: www.marshallcavendish.us

© Times Media Private Limited 1997
© Marshall Cavendish International (Asia) Private Limited 2010
® "Cultures of the World" is a registered trademark of Times Publishing Limited.

Originated and designed by Marshall Cavendish International (Asia) Private Limited
An imprint of Marshall Cavendish International (Asia) Private Limited
A member of Times Publishing Limited

Marshall Cavendish is a trademark of Times Publishing Limited.

All Internet sites were correct and accurate at the time of printing. All monetary figures in this publication are in U.S. dollars.

Library of Congress Cataloging-in-Publication Data
O'Shea, Maria.
  Kuwait / by Maria O'Shea and Michael Spilling. — 2nd ed.
    p. cm. — (Cultures of the world)
  Summary: "Provides comprehensive information on the geography, history, wildlife, governmental structure, economy, cultural diversity, peoples, religion, and culture of Kuwait"—Provided by publisher.
  ISBN 978-0-7614-4479-4
  1. Kuwait—Juvenile literature. I. Spilling, Michael. II. Title.

DS247.K8O7 2010
  953.67--dc22   2009007069

Printed in China
7 6 5 4 3 2 1

CONTENTS

INTRODUCTION

SLIGHTLY SMALLER THAN THE STATE OF NEW JERSEY, KUWAIT is home to ancient civilizations and part of one of the most fought-over corners of the modern world. Kuwait's land is mainly flat desert blessed with plentiful supplies of oil, from which the modern state of Kuwait has become prosperous. The capital, Kuwait City, is an oasis of modern technology in an otherwise arid landscape, full of museums, restaurants, modern shopping complexes, international hotels, and luxury beach resorts. Despite bordering much larger and more powerful neighbors—Iraq and Saudi Arabia—Kuwait has forged an identity of its own built around the ruling emir and careful investment of its oil wealth in public projects. It is this prosperity that made Kuwait a target for invasion by Iraq in 1990. Although Kuwaitis have, over time, learned to put the traumas of the invasion behind them, the country still shows the scars of the Iraqi occupation today. *Cultures of the World: Kuwait* explores this small, commercially successful and forward-looking country in one of the most volatile regions of the world.

GEOGRAPHY

A camel in the desert. The climate in Kuwait is dry and harsh.

CHAPTER 1

Kuwait has
a harsh and
unforgiving
desert climate,
with little
rainfall. Most
of the country's
population is
concentrated in
its cities.

KUWAIT LIES AT THE NORTHWEST corner of the long, narrow waters of the Persian, or Arabian, Gulf. To the east it is bounded by the Gulf, to the north and west by Iraq, and to the south and southwest by the vast kingdom of Saudi Arabia.

Kuwait has nine islands, of which the most important ones, in terms of oil reserves and archaeological sites, are Bubiyan and Faylaka. In the south lies the Neutral or Divided Zone, which is about 2,200 square miles (5,700 square km), between Kuwait and Saudi Arabia. This was partitioned in 1969, and Kuwait administers the northern portion.

Kuwait is a very small country surrounded by much larger neighbors. From the north to the south it extends 124 miles (200 km) and from the east to the west 106 miles (170 km). Only in the east does Kuwait have no immediate neighbor, although the Persian Gulf is bounded by other, larger states.

Right: The waters of the Arabian Gulf provide an important source of drinking water for Kuwaitis once it is desalinized.

DESERT AND SEASHORE

Kuwait can be divided into four geographic zones: the desert plateau in the west; a desert plain, covering most of the country; salt marshes and saline depressions that cover most of Kuwait Bay; and an eastern area of coastal dunes. The country consists of a gently undulating desert that gradually rises away from the sea to a maximum height of 475 feet (145 m) in the northwest and 951 feet (290 m) in the east.

The terrain varies from firm clay and gravel in the north to loose sandy ground in the south. The plain is an arid steppe desert, and except in the northeast, there are few sand dunes. There are no rivers, lakes, or mountains, but the flatness is relieved by shallow depressions and a few low hills, such as Ahmadi Hill at 450 feet (137 m) in the south and Jal Az-Zor Ridge at 476 feet (145 m) on the north side of Kuwait Bay. The coastline in the north and around Kuwait Bay consists mainly of mudflats, while there are many fine beaches in the south.

The Persian Gulf separates Kuwait and the other Arab Gulf states from Iran in the north. Since the Iran-Iraq War, however, many Arabs prefer to call it the Arabian Gulf. The U.S. State Department calls it the Persian Gulf, but many diplomats feel it is safer to refer to the sea, as well as the region, as the Gulf.

The Arabian Gulf beachfront.

NOMADS AND BORDERS

As there are no mountains, rivers, or other natural obstacles, Kuwait was for a long time a transit area for nomadic tribes known as bedouin whose caravans moved freely over the desert. This made it difficult to agree on the boundaries separating the countries in the area. There was much dispute over this, resulting—much later—in boundary problems with Saudi Arabia and Iraq.

In 1922 the British negotiated an agreement on the Kuwaiti-Saudi Arabia border. This led to the creation of a compromise neutral zone, which was formally divided between the two countries in 1969. Kuwait's northern border with Iraq was agreed upon in 1923, but Iraqi claims on Kuwaiti territory continued: first in 1938, the year oil was discovered in Kuwait, and again in 1961, when Britain recognized Kuwait's independence.

CLIMATE AND WEATHER

The climate of Kuwait is typical of the desert regions but is modified by its coastline, which is 310 miles (499 km) long. Summers are long, hot, and

Tents in the desert in al-Mutla.

Kuwait Bay is one of two generous-size natural harbors in the northern half of the Arabian Gulf; the other is in Bahrain. It has always been a prime access point for trade entering and leaving the hinterland of northeast Saudi Arabia and Iraq. Before oil was discovered, it was the country's most valuable resource, and as the location of Kuwait's main commercial port, its economic importance continues.

dry, with a daily average temperature of 110°F (43°C). Winters are short and cool, occasionally cold, with rare sudden showers and dust storms. During fall, temperatures start to decrease to the lower 80s°F (28°C) throughout October and the upper to mid-60s°F (20°C) in November. During the winter months, from November to February, the average temperature is 55°F (13°C). Even at this time of year, daytime temperatures can rise to 80°F (27°C), although they can drop as low as 35°F (2°C) if there is night frost. In the spring months, throughout the afternoons clouds build up seemingly from nowhere, bringing occasional thunderstorms by the evening. Directional winds are seasonal: hot and dry from the north, and warm and humid from the south.

Rainfall is unpredictable, from as little as 0.8 inch (2 cm) in one year to as much as 13.8 inches (35 cm) in another, though the average is less than 3.2 inches (8 cm) annually. Dust storms occur throughout the year but are more common in the spring and summer. Humidity is usually low, except in the late summer. The highest recorded temperature was 125°F (52°C) in July

Many birds stop in Kuwait during their seasonal migrations.

THE SEASONS IN KUWAIT

Spring

Early spring	February 16 to April 8	Mild and pleasant, cool at night
Midspring	April 9 to May 13	Very changeable
Late spring	May 14 to May 20	Getting warmer, with hot winds

Summer

Transitional	May 21 to June 5	Temperatures rise
Dry period	June 6 to July 19	Very hot, with scorching winds and sandstorms
Humid period	July 20 to August 31	Temperatures peak but humidity rises
Transitional	September 1 to November 4	Temperatures drop but humidity is high

Fall	November 5 to December 5	Mild and pleasant, sometimes cloudy, cool at night

Winter	December 6 to February 15	Cold, northwesterly winds, cloudy with occasional rain

1978, making Kuwait the fourth hottest place in the world, and the lowest was 25°F (-4°C) in January 1964. Daily fluctuation is wide, especially in the desert, where the nights can be very cold, even in summer.

HARDLY A DROP TO DRINK

The lack of fresh drinking water has always been a serious problem in Kuwait. There are few naturally occurring water sources. The water is mostly brackish, though it can be used for irrigation and cleaning. Even before the oil era, clean drinking water was imported from Iraq. A good

Although modern farming techniques are costly, vegetable farming in Wafra helps to reduce the country's dependence on imports of food.

domestic source of drinking water was not discovered until the late 1950s, at al-Rawdatain and Umm al-Aish in the north. This underground reservoir contains possibly 48 billion gallons (182 billion l) and is the only source of freshwater in the country. The bulk of Kuwait's water comes from the sea and is processed at desalination plants near Mina Abdullah to make it fit to drink. In 2008 a contract was awarded for a new desalination plant with more-efficient technologies to be completed by 2010.

WHEN THE DESERT BLOOMS

A land of deserts, oil wells, and cities, Kuwait uses barely 1 percent of its land for farming.

Although vegetable gardens were once cultivated on parts of the coastal strip, and date palms and fruit trees were once the pride of al-Jahrah, at the western end of Kuwait Bay, farming has always been very marginal to the economy. The immense effort involved in farming in such arid conditions, using limited water supplies, means it is cheaper to import most food. As the Kuwaiti government is much concerned about the country's dependence on the outside world, some areas of the desert have been irrigated, and farming is practiced at a great financial cost, notably in Wafra, Sulaibiya, and Abdali.

Flora in Kuwait is sparse, since there is little regular rain. The soil is mostly sandy and often salty. The desert is scattered with patches of coarse, weedy grass and small bell-shape bushes. The country has up to 400 types of vegetation, and a good rainfall in winter can produce an abundant growth of lush green grass and wildflowers; these quickly wither and die, however.

ANIMAL LIFE

The desert contains many rodents, lizards, and other small animals, but the rabbits, wolves, and gazelles that once roamed the desert have been hunted to near extinction. There is some pasture for sheep, goats, and camels. These animals may appear to wander wild, but they actually belong to the bedouin tribes. Although Kuwait has only 20 native species of birds, mostly larks, more than 300 types of birds pass through in the spring and the fall on their annual migration, using Kuwait as a stop-off point. These include flamingos, steppe eagles, cormorants, and bee-eaters. At certain times of the year pink flamingos can be seen on the salt flats to the north of Kuwait City.

The waters of the Gulf are very salty and warm, with temperatures ranging from 54°F to 97°F (12°C to 36°C). More than 200 species of fish and other sea animals can be found in the local waters, including dolphins, porpoises, whales, and sea snakes. Many types of shellfish can be found along the shores of Kuwait, as well as in the beds deep under the sea.

KUWAITI CITIES

With its small size and a population of almost 2,597,000, Kuwait has a population density of 364 people per square mile (140.6 per square km), more than four times that of the United States. More than 90 percent of the population of Kuwait live along a coastal belt about 6 miles (10 km) wide, stretching from al-Jahrah at the western edge of Kuwait Bay to Mina Abdullah in the south. This is known as the metropolitan area.

Kuwait has selected a national flower from its indigenous flora, the Arfaj flower, which is rare in many countries. It covers 30 percent of Kuwait's surface area throughout the year.

The rest of Kuwait is only very sparsely populated. In recent years the Kuwaiti government has built cities in the west, the northeast, and the south to absorb the population increase and to relieve the pressure on the metropolitan area. The population of Kuwait grows by 3.6 percent per year, mostly due to incoming expatriates—foreigners who come to the country for work. Of the nine islands of Kuwait, only Faylaka is inhabited. The nearly 6,000 people who live on the island are supplied with electricity and water by underwater pipes and cables from Kuwait City. This island is a well-developed tourist resort, accessible by boat from the mainland.

The main cities are Kuwait City, located on the site of the original fort settlement at the southwestern tip of Kuwait Bay; al-Jahrah, an old agricultural town to the west; and al-Salmiya, to the east of the bay. These cities and the southern coastal cities of Mina al-Ahmadi and Mina Abdullah are linked and encircled by a network of more than 3,037 miles (4,887 km) of expressways. The total area of the Kuwait City metro area is 77.2 square miles (200 square km). Only five other populated areas really exist outside of the metropolitan area: the oil towns of al-Abdaliya,

An aerial view of Kuwait City.

RESIDENTIAL ZONES

After independence all citizens were granted free housing. The residential areas of Kuwait City were allocated according to tribal, racial, and religious groups. So it is that certain areas are inhabited by Shiite Muslims, others by Sunni Muslims, and still others by bedouin tribes. The various immigrant communities were also allocated housing in distinct districts. All 16 residential zones have their own social amenities, such as shopping malls, mosques, libraries, health centers, banks, restaurants, and cafés. This urban lifestyle thus reinforces the tribal, class, racial, and religious divisions that exist in Kuwait.

al-Subayhiyah, and Wafra and the ports of al-Khiran and Mina Saud, all to the south and west.

The area originally known as Kuwait City, which is the seat of the government, is a small parcel of land, just 1,999 acres (809 ha), or one-tenth the size of New York's Manhattan Island. The emir's palace and most offices of banks and investment firms are found here. The city and its suburbs have been rebuilt since the 1950s in a series of master plans. The area was zoned into business and residential areas divided by ring roads, which expand outward in concentric circles.

MINA AL-AHMADI, THRIVING IN THE DESERT

Mina al-Ahmadi was Kuwait's first oil town, founded more than 50 years ago. Although it now lies in the metropolitan area, it is still noted for its greenery, pleasant gardens, and villas on tree-lined avenues. Before Kuwait City's massive expansion and the construction of the expressway, Mina al-Ahmadi was a 45-minute car journey across the desert from the capital. It was a popular place to spend a relaxing day picnicking in the parks. The town was founded by the Kuwait Oil Company, and the green surroundings were considered to be essential for the morale of employees. Today the port acts a major refueling base for U.S. commercial and military shipping.

Expatriates make up two-thirds of Kuwait's population of 2,596,799.

HISTORY

The ruins of a Greek or Alexandrian settlement on Kuwait's Faylaka Island.

KUWAIT IS A VERY NEW COUNTRY, having received independence from Britain only in 1961, and yet, compared with many of their neighbors, Kuwaitis have a long-standing and well-developed sense of their unique identity. This is partly due to formal attempts by the government to fashion such an identity and also to the nature of the country's past.

Despite its short history Kuwait has always been relatively independent and distinct from its neighbors. Its traditional dependence on trade with the rest of the world and on pearl diving ensured that Kuwaitis were exposed to many cultures, and this helped foster a distinct identity as well as enriching Kuwaiti culture.

The trading and seafaring life meant that men could be absent for up to a half-year; those left behind became dependent on each other for support. This created a powerful sense of community, which at least partially survived the oil boom.

Right: The Iraqi invasion led to much destruction in Kuwait.

A dhow under construction at a Kuwaiti harbor.

Kuwaiti history was one of almost uninterrupted economic success until the Iraqi invasion of 1990. Despite the devastation visited upon Kuwait's oil industry and infrastructure by the invasion, Kuwait has since recovered from the effects of the Iraqi army occupation to become a stable, comfortable, and prosperous country once again.

Wealth generated from trading has given way to wealth from oil and investments, but the same groups of tribes and families have continued to profit. To a large extent Kuwaiti history is also that of certain families who founded the country 300 years ago and continue to govern it in the face of increasing challenges and growing Western influence.

OLD KUWAIT

Three hundred and fifty years ago Kuwait City was an uninhabited headland jutting into the northwest corner of the Persian Gulf. The town of Kuwait was built in 1672 by the Bani Khalid, the dominant tribe of northeastern Arabia in the early 18th century. It was called Grane until the mid-19th century. *Kuwait* is a diminutive of the word *kut* (kuht), meaning "castle" or "fort." A scattering of nomadic families lived along the shore with their camels. Internal disputes and waning influence over the region eventually caused the Bani Khalid clan to decline, allowing the Bani Utub to rise to power.

The Bani Utub tribe, a loosely connected group of interrelated families from central Arabia, arrived in Kuwait in the early 18th century. Famine had forced them to migrate in the late 17th century, traveling to Kuwait via Qatar. Once settled in Kuwait they lived by pearl diving, boatbuilding, and trading. The settlement became an important port of call for the desert caravans transporting Indian goods from the Persian Gulf to Aleppo in Syria. By the end of the 19th century, the town had a population of 10,000 people. A majority of the men were involved in seafaring trades.

Archaeologists believe that Faylaka was a holy island, possibly a place of pilgrimage 3,000 years ago for the Sumerians of Mesopotamia, a land that now constitutes the greater part of Iraq. When Faylaka was discovered by one of Alexander the Great's generals, its sanctuary and shrines to Artemis, the goddess of hunting, were noted. The island contains Kuwait's richest archaeological sites, with Greek temples and fortresses and three Bronze Age settlements.

Alexander the Great conquered most of the Middle East before his death at the age of 33 in 323 B.C. Greek historians described the many journeys of Alexander the Great and his companions, including the establishment of a garrison on an island in the Persian Gulf named Icarus; this occurred shortly before Alexander's death. From archaeological explorations carried out in the 1960s, it is believed that the Kuwaiti island of Faylaka is the legendary island of Icarus. Although Alexander died three days before his planned conquest of Arabia, Icarus remained an outpost of the successor Seleucid kingdom, which was based in Syria. During this time it prospered as a trading center, until it was overrun by the Parthians, becoming part of Persia but ceasing to have any importance.

KUWAIT DEVELOPS AS A CITY-STATE

By the mid-18th century the al-Sabah family had become Kuwait's political rulers, a position it still holds. Family members were responsible for political functions, such as diplomatic and tribal relations and security, while other families handled economic and trading matters. Kuwait's small size meant that diplomacy and manipulation of local power balances were necessary to keep a degree of independence from the surrounding powers. Thus the al-Sabah family was able to establish a strong power base at the expense of the other tribes. In 1756 the Bani Utub elected Sabah I bin Jaber (Sabah I) as the first emir of Kuwait.

Until World War I, Kuwait, like the rest of the Arabian Peninsula and the Arab world, was part of the Ottoman Empire's sphere of influence, ruled from Istanbul, Turkey. In the late 19th century the Ottomans added most of the Gulf coastal regions to the province of Basra, including Kuwait in 1871.

THE CARAVAN TRADE

A caravan, with as many as 5,000 camels, could travel from Kuwait to Aleppo in Syria in 70 days. The sheikh of Kuwait could arrange for these caravans to travel safely, without the risk of a raid by bedouin bandits, within the town of Kuwait and beyond. The city grew as new trades sprang up to serve the travelers and to meet the needs of the bedouin who visited the town souks, or markets, and the needs of the townspeople themselves.

The al-Sabah agreed to this, despite having ruled Kuwait for 150 years, as long as the ruler was given the title of governor and the al-Sabah were allowed to continue to govern the country.

BRITAIN AND KUWAIT

At about this time the British became interested in Iraq and the Gulf, as it was an important staging post on the way to India, which was one of the most important parts of the British Empire.

A regular steamship service between Basra and Bombay called at Kuwait, and British Indian postal services were available to traders. British interest in the area provided the Kuwaiti rulers with a way to free themselves of Ottoman control, and in 1899 Sheikh Mubarak al-Sabah signed an agreement with Britain. In return for British protection Kuwait agreed not to dispose of any part of its territory or enter into any relationship with any power other than Britain. In 1913 the borders of Kuwait, the Arabian region known as Nejd, and the province of Basra were defined. Britain was in control, and the al-Sabah family had to tread carefully to maintain any independence.

WARTIME PROMISES

During World War I, Kuwait was occupied by British forces, who were fighting against Ottoman Turkey for control of the Middle East. In return the British promised the Kuwaitis an independent state after the war. At the end of the

There is archaeological evidence that the inhabitants of Faylaka Island in the Persian Gulf had connections with Mesopotamia and the trading center of Dilmun (modern Bahrain) as far back as 1200 B.C. No records exist, however, to tell us about the period between then and 323 B.C., when Alexander the Great landed on the island.

PEARLING

A pearl is a translucent ball formed inside a shellfish. When a piece of grit or sand enters the shell, the shellfish coats it with the glossy mother-of-pearl (calcium carbonate) with which it lines its shells, forming a pearl. Natural pearls are usually cream colored but can be of many shades, including black, green, and blue. They vary in shape and size and at times have been more valuable on the world market than diamonds. This is partly because of the difficulties involved in collecting the pearls. The mother-of-pearl inside the shell can be used to make buttons and other decorative items.

Pearl divers would stuff beeswax into their ears, close their nostrils with a horn pincer, and protect their fingers with leather covers. They would then leap from their boats, a rock tied to their ankle to pull them to the seabed, and gather as many oysters into a basket as they could before they had to come up for air. About 20 oysters could be collected in the 40—75 seconds that they stayed under. A good diver could dive up to 50 times a day, although it could take many dives to find even one pearl. There was no way to predict the presence of a pearl in a shellfish, so the divers had to depend on their luck in getting the ones with the precious finds. Pearl oysters are not edible, so those without pearls are useless. The divers were not paid a salary but took a share of the profits from the summer pearling voyages, which might travel as far as southern India, where there are large pearl banks.

The work was dangerous—a diver would start at a very young age, when he was very fit, then retire early due to breathing problems, unless he had already been injured or killed by sharks. As the diver had to borrow money in advance from the ship's captain to support his family during the journey, he was already in debt and under pressure to dive many times. The daily routine was long and the food frugal, consisting mostly of coffee and dates, with some fish. In 1904 Kuwait had about 500 pearl-diving crews, providing a living for more than 9,000 men.

Cultured pearls are produced by introducing small beads into the shells of oysters living in specially created tanks. Such pearls were known in China for centuries. In the early 20th century world prices of pearls fell because of an increasing Japanese production of cultured pearls. Although they are less valuable, cultured pearls are extremely easy, cheap, and safe to produce.

war and with the collapse of the Ottoman Empire, the British and the French divided up the Middle East. Kuwait remained under British protection. The British gained the sole right to exploit Kuwait's oil. A special relationship continued between Britain and Kuwait until 1961, when Kuwait became officially independent. During the next 30 years, Kuwait's oil revenues allowed it to rapidly develop into a modern, comfortable Gulf state.

BACKGROUND TO THE IRAQI INVASION

The Iraqi invasion of Kuwait in 1990 came about because of a contested history and Kuwait's wealth. The personality and style of Iraq's leader, Saddam Hussein, was also a factor. First, the Iraqis considered the international boundaries of the Arab countries to have been imposed by the colonialist Europeans who had occupied the Middle East after World War I. In particular, Iraqis felt Kuwait should rightly be part of Iraq, not only because of historic trading links but also because bedouin tribes had always moved between the two countries before the creation of national boundaries.

Second, Iraq needed more money to pay for the damage caused by eight years of war with Iran (1980—88). The rights to certain oil fields straddling the Iraq-Kuwait boundary were unresolved, and Iraq wanted more oil to sell. The Kuwaitis had also made a lot of oil available on the world market, which caused the price to drop. Iraq had asked Kuwait to reduce the amount of oil it sold in order to raise oil prices, but Kuwait refused. The Kuwaitis also wanted Iraq to repay the loans incurred when Iraq was at war with Iran. Throughout the summer of 1990, Kuwait and Iraq argued about oil production and prices, the disputed oil fields, and loan repayments. As efforts to resolve the dispute foundered, the Iraqis moved troops and weapons to the Kuwaiti border.

IRAQ INVADES

Iraqi president Saddam Hussein had invaded Iran before, in 1980. Officially that had been over a border dispute, and Iraq had received, if not open support, at least no retaliatory action from the United States or the United Nations.

Oil in Kuwait has fueled many social changes. In 1936 there were two primary schools in Kuwait; by 1947 there were 19, and by 1958, 30,000 children attended more than 90 schools. In 1961 Kuwait had very few college graduates; by 1966 it had its own university. Today more than 500,000 students are enrolled in schools in Kuwait.

PEARLS TO OIL

Pearls were the oil of earlier times, providing Kuwait's main source of income. In the 1930s, however, the pearling industry went into a decline caused by two factors: The Japanese had developed a method of artificial pearl cultivation, and a worldwide economic depression meant a dramatic fall in the demand for pearls in Europe and the United States. By 1945 only five pearling boats were still working in Kuwait out of the 500 active boats at the turn of the century.

Fortunately oil came to the rescue. Oil was discovered in 1938, and oil exploitation began in earnest after World War II ended. By 1957 Kuwait was the second-largest oil exporter in the world, exceeded only by Venezuela. As one of the world's least populated countries, with fewer than 250,000 people, Kuwait was set to become one of the wealthiest.

The oil boom was overseen by the emir, Sheikh Abdullah III al-Salim al-Sabah, who died four years after Kuwait's independence in 1961. He transformed the country into a modern state and dramatically improved social conditions.

This past experience, as well as a conversation with the U.S. ambassador to Iraq, led Hussein to think that another Iraqi invasion would be the best solution to his problems with Kuwait and would not meet with any serious objection from the U.S. Most Iraqis felt Kuwaitis were too wealthy and that they should be forced to share that wealth more.

In the middle of the night on August 2, 1990, Iraqi soldiers and tanks swept into Kuwait. Kuwait's army totaled only 17,000 soldiers with little experience, while the Iraqi army of 1 million soldiers had the experience of almost a decade of war with Iran.

By morning Iraqi troops controlled Kuwait City. The emir of Kuwait and his close family escaped to Saudi Arabia. Despite a UN resolution asking Iraq to withdraw, the Iraqis proclaimed a transitional government. Within a week American troops began to arrive in Saudi Arabia, as it was feared that Iraq would extend its invasion to Saudi Arabia. In response, President Hussein declared Kuwait the 19th province of Iraq. Several Arab states joined forces with the United States to set up Operation Desert Shield,

Allied troops arrive in Saudi Arabia as the Gulf crisis deepens after the Iraqi invasion of Kuwait.

involving 250,000 soldiers, including 200,000 Americans. The operations were aimed at defending Saudi Arabia and encouraging Iraq to withdraw peacefully from Kuwait.

Inside Kuwait the civilian population was terrorized, and those who resisted were tortured and executed under a harsh military regime. Economic sanctions against Iraq were not working, and people became even more fearful that Iraq's apparent success in Kuwait would embolden it to attack Saudi Arabia. Allied troop strength in Saudi Arabia was increased to 550,000, including 350,000 Americans, while Iraqi forces in Kuwait rose to 600,000.

By January 1991 a diplomatic solution appeared impossible, so on January 17 the allied forces began Operation Desert Storm—a devastating air campaign against Iraq and occupied Kuwait. On February 24 the ground assault began, and the coalition forces entered both Kuwait and southern Iraq. Within two days the allied troops had reoccupied Kuwait City, and at 8:00 A.M. on February 28, after 100 hours of fighting, a cease-fire was called. Kuwait paid the coalition forces $17 billion for their help.

Kuwaiti air force A-4 Skyhawk attack planes preparing to fly.

A NEW KUWAIT?

Many hoped that the end of the war would see a number of changes in the Arab world and the Gulf states, including a greater degree of democracy. Restoring law and order in Kuwait was difficult. Suspected collaborators—especially expatriate Palestinians—were sought out and punished. It took less than a year to extinguish the burning oil wells, but for more than two years land mines were still being discovered. Since the war all Kuwaitis have been concerned with rebuilding the country and the leadership with meeting the changed demands of the population.

THE AFTERMATH OF WAR

Kuwait's infrastructure was badly damaged by the Iraqi occupation and the war. Looting was widespread. Goods such as hospital equipment, cars, computers, and valuables were carted away to Iraq, as were antiquities from the museums. Very few houses escaped the looting, and most public offices and facilities, such as schools and the university, were stripped of their contents and wrecked. Many buildings were badly damaged, and the desalination plants, which provide most of Kuwait's water, needed to be rebuilt, as did the airport and the harbors. Bomb damage to the oil installations caused a huge oil slick that harmed marine life and the fishing industry. The Iraqis set fire to 600 of the 950 oil wells in the country; the smoke polluted the whole Gulf region.

Most of the people who had stayed behind during the invasion were those who did not have Kuwaiti citizenship, such as the Palestinians, and were afraid to leave in case they would not be allowed to return. After the war, expatriates who were thought to have collaborated with the Iraqis were summarily expelled or refused reentry. Even those who were not found to be collaborators but who had remained in Kuwait during the occupation

Iraqi tanks driving along a boulevard in Kuwait City.

HOW THE IRAQI INVASION AFFECTED WOMEN

The Iraqi invasion affected the entire region, especially in challenging traditional views of women's roles in society. Kuwaiti women under the occupation were active in the resistance. Also the American women who served in the U.S. Army were highly conspicuous in this conservative region, providing an example to the local women of a different way of living. At the same time, the Kuwaiti women in exile in Saudi Arabia were seen by the local women there as having more freedom. For example, unlike Saudi women, Kuwaiti women are allowed to drive cars and work alongside men. This led to demonstrations by educated Saudi women for more freedom.

came under suspicion and were expelled or deprived of their residency rights. The Palestinians were singled out for harsh treatment because the Palestinian political leadership had supported the Iraqi government. Without the Palestinians, Kuwait was deprived of a highly skilled and educated workforce.

After liberation Kuwaitis worked together to restore the country to some degree of normality. More than $5 billion were spent on rebuilding and restoring the country, especially repairing the damage to the oil infrastructure. The elections in 1992 were widely interpreted as a success for the supporters of increased Islamic law. They were a disappointment to liberals, including those who supported extending suffrage to women, who were not to receive that right until 2005.

In 2003 Kuwait served as the major staging base for the U.S.-led invasion of Iraq. As a close American ally, Kuwait was the only Arab nation to publicly support the invasion. Today Kuwait remains an important transit route for coalition forces and civilians going to and from Iraq.

After the death of Sheikh Jaber III al-Ahmad al-Jaber al-Sabah in January 2006, the then-prime minister, Sheikh Sabah IV al-Ahmad al-Sabah, was elected emir of Kuwait. He was chosen over his elderly cousin, Sheikh Saad al-Abdullah, who despite being directly in line for the throne was too ill and frail to take up the position.

GOVERNMENT

Women awaiting their turn at the polling station.

THE STATE OF KUWAIT, or Dawlat al-Kuwayt in Arabic, is a constitutional monarchy, ruled by the emir of Kuwait, who by law must be from the al-Sabah family, descended from the late Mubarak al-Sabah.

The emir rules with the help of an elected National Assembly, a Council of Ministers selected by the prime minister and approved by the emir, and the bureaucracy. The emir appoints the prime minister. To a large extent these institutions have been successful in creating a national identity that includes loyalty to the country's leaders. The government has generally encouraged the people of Kuwait to support the "national

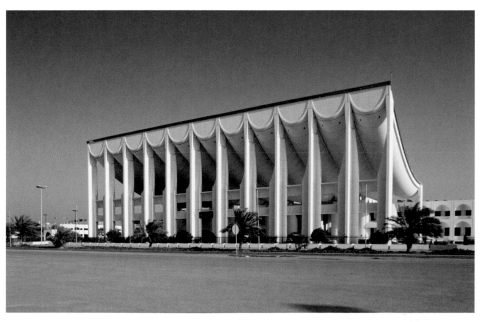
The Kuwait National Assembly Building.

29

Kuwaitis shopping at a night market. In terms of representation, not many of the people in Kuwait have the right to vote.

interest" rather than used force. The government has over the decades faced opposition from liberals and Islamists, but disagreements have largely been resolved peacefully.

THE NATIONAL ASSEMBLY

Kuwait was the first Arab Gulf country to have an elected parliament, the National Assembly.

The National Assembly is considered one of the strongest parliaments in the Gulf today, and it sometimes expresses differences of opinion with the cabinet in a robust fashion. From its establishment after independence, the 50 elected members of the National Assembly carried on a lively political debate with the government until it was closed between 1976 and 1981 and then from 1986 until elections were held in 1992, following the end of the Iraqi occupation. Political parties have not been legalized in Kuwait, although National Assembly members have formed opposing groups with certain interests.

Parliament in session.

The right to vote was originally restricted to Kuwaiti men. In 2005, however, the National Assembly passed legislation allowing women to vote and run for parliament for the first time in Kuwait's history. In addition, all Kuwaiti citizens over 21 years of age can now vote, except for active members of the armed forces and the police, who are also barred from serving in the National Assembly. In 1985 only 57,000 Kuwaitis, fewer than 5 percent of the total residential population of 1.5 million, could vote. In elections held in 2006 more than 340,000 Kuwaitis, including about 195,000 women, were eligible to vote for 253 candidates, including 28 women. The many foreign workers in Kuwait cannot vote.

The first National Assembly frequently criticized the cabinet ministers and government policies, setting a precedent for future assemblies. As the number of disagreements grew, the emir dissolved the assembly in 1976. He was particularly concerned with the ties that seemed to be developing

Although the al-Sabah family has ruled Kuwait since the 18th century, the family has ruled as a formal institution only since the mid-20th century. Since independence, the ruling family has always held at least one-quarter of all cabinet posts and the most important ministerial posts such as foreign affairs, defense, information, and the interior. There are more than 1,200 members of the al-Sabah family, who are themselves divided into various groups depending on their closeness to the ruling line, the descendants of the first emir's sons, Jabir and Salem.

between the Kuwaiti opposition and groups in the wider Arab world, especially considering the large number of politically active, highly educated Palestinians who were living in Kuwait. Kuwait's neighbor, Saudi Arabia, had never approved of the democratic experiment in Kuwait and encouraged the emir to be wary of possible challenges to his rule.

The emir claimed that the members of the National Assembly had spent so much time arguing over issues that budgets and new laws were delayed. Certainly the members had made many enemies from their campaigns against corruption and price controls, campaigns that were popular with the people. When the assembly was dissolved, press controls were also introduced.

To the surprise of many, the emir kept his promise to restore the National Assembly at a time that he judged right, and this happened in 1981. The 1979 Iranian revolution concerned the emir, as it demonstrated the dangers of too little democracy and the inability of a strong government to control a dissatisfied population. By encouraging Islamist candidates to stand for the National Assembly, the emir hoped to include the religious opposition in the government. Excluding them, as Iran had done, could lead to a revolutionary opposition. In the elections held in 2003, 2006, and 2008, Islamic parties have made steady gains and maintained a substantial presence in the National Assembly.

Most residents of Kuwait are not citizens and so do not have the right to vote. Kuwaiti law gives citizenship to those who are descended in the male line from residents of Kuwait dating back to 1920.

Supporters of the Orange Movement.

RECENT ELECTIONS

In the most recent elections, held in May 2008, a loose alliance of reformists and Islamists gained roughly two-thirds of the parliamentary seats. In these elections 361,685 Kuwaitis were eligible to vote, more than half of them women. Although 27 of the 275 candidates were women, none of the female candidates won a seat. New rules were introduced in this election: Instead of 25 constituencies electing two candidates each, five constituencies elected 10 candidates each. This was a demand of the reformist Kuwaiti Orange Movement, which led mass demonstrations and a parliamentary walkout after the 2006 election due to suspicions of vote buying and electoral fraud. The reformists had argued that a larger number of smaller constituencies made corruption and vote buying easier for powerful political parties.

ISLAMISTS AND LIBERALS

Liberal political groups in Kuwait hoped that Saddam Hussein's removal from power in 2003 by the U.S.-led coalition would strengthen their

Although women candidates ran in two elections since being granted the right to run for the National Assembly, they have yet to win a seat.

The current emir of Kuwait is Sheikh Sabah IV al-Ahmad al-Jaber al-Sabah (born June 6, 1929). He was sworn in on January 29, 2006, after confirmation by the National Assembly. He is the fourth son of the late Sheikh Ahmad al-Jaber al-Sabah, a former emir of Kuwait and head of the ruling al-Sabah family. Half-brother of a previous emir, Sheikh Jaber III al-Ahmad al-Jaber al-Sabah, Sheikh Sabah had served as the prime minister from July 2003 until his appointment as emir in 2006. Before that he had served as the foreign minister of Kuwait from 1963 to 2003, making him one of the longest-serving foreign ministers in the world. Sheikh Sabah became the new emir after the then-crown prince, Sheikh Saad al-Sabah, was too ill to take up the position. This caused a constitutional crisis that was resolved only when the National Assembly intervened and pressured the ruling family into choosing Sheikh Sabah as the new emir.

Sheikh Sabah has overseen some groundbreaking legislation. He has supported women's right to vote as well as introduced laws upholding press freedoms rarely seen elsewhere in the Arab world.

> ## EMIRS OF KUWAIT SINCE INDEPENDENCE

Sheikh Abdullah III al-Salim al-Sabah: January 29, 1950—November 24, 1965

Sheikh Sabah III al-Salim al-Sabah: November 24, 1965—December 31, 1977

Sheikh Jaber III al-Ahmad al-Jaber al-Sabah: December 31, 1977— January 15, 2006

Sheikh Saad al-Abdullah al-Salim al-Sabah: January 15, 2006—January 24, 2006

Sheikh Sabah IV al-Ahmad al-Jaber al-Sabah: January 29, 2006—present

efforts to modernize the country. However, in the elections held in 2003, 2006, and 2008, traditionalist and Islamist parties made steady gains. Islamic parties won 22 seats in the 50-seat National Assembly in 2006 and 24 seats in 2008.

Islamic groupings include the Islamic Salafi Alliance and the Islamic Constitutional Movement (ICM). These groups seek the introduction of sharia, or Islamic, law and oppose women's suffrage.

By contrast, liberal groups such as the National Democratic Alliance (NDA) believe that Kuwait should abide first and foremost by the laws of its constitution. The NDA campaigned for the political empowerment of women and stresses the importance of uniting Kuwaiti citizens under the umbrella of nationalism rather than dividing them into sects, tribes, and religious groupings. Many young Kuwaitis support the NDA. Two Shiite groups, the National Islamic Alliance and the Justice and Peace Alliance, represent Kuwait's substantial Shiite community.

THE BUREAUCRACY

The Kuwaiti bureaucracy, which expanded rapidly after the discovery of oil, is one of the largest in the world for a country its size. Kuwait did not have an extensive administration under the British, and oil exploitation makes few bureaucratic demands. The need to spend the oil revenues was the real impetus to expanding this bureaucracy. The system provided pleasant employment for Kuwaitis, who were no longer required in the traditional industries that were displaced by oil wealth.

Islamists are those who believe that the country should be run as an Islamic state, according to the guidance of the Koran and Islamic law.

The army is well funded but lacks soldiers, despite national conscription.

As there have never been enough educated Kuwaitis to run this giant organization, many Arabs from other countries, in particular Palestinians, were employed in managerial positions, overseen by Kuwaiti managers or ministers. By 1989 only 44 percent of civil servants were Kuwaiti. At the senior-staff level the percentage of Kuwaitis was higher, at 66 percent, after efforts were made to increase the proportion. This was an overrepresentation of Kuwaitis in the civil service, as only 28 percent of the population were Kuwaiti citizens at that time. According to recent statistics, the Kuwaiti government employs 311,000 Kuwaitis in government jobs. Most citizens working in the government sector are in desk jobs or are firefighters or police.

Kuwait is divided into five electoral regions, each of which elects 10 members to the National Assembly. A Council of Ministers is appointed by the prime minister and approved by the emir. The current prime minister is Nasir Muhammad al-Ahmad al-Sabah, who was appointed in April 2007.

THE MILITARY

Kuwait has always depended on diplomacy to solve problems with its neighbors. The army was intended merely to delay an aggressor while the government rallied diplomatic support. In 1978 Kuwait was the first Gulf state to introduce national conscription and compulsory high school military training. All Kuwaiti men, including members of the al-Sabah family, between the ages of 18 and 30 had to serve in the army. Previously the army had relied on bedouin, many of whom were not citizens, assisted by expatriate advisers. In 1980 the Iran-Iraq War led to a call-up of Kuwaiti men up to the age of 50. Despite attempts to make army life more attractive, Kuwaitis were reluctant to serve. On the eve of the Iraqi invasion, the army was only 20,000 strong, mostly non-Kuwaitis, and up to 60 percent of them were on summer leave.

Since the war, Kuwait has modernized and increased the size of its armed forces, mainly with the help of the U.S. military. The government has also sought to improve defense arrangements with other Arab states. Today Kuwait's armed forces are approximately 50,000 strong and maintain more than 300 main battle tanks to deter invasion from aggressive neighbors. A separately organized national guard maintains security within the country, while police forces are under civil control. Women have been able to serve in the police forces since 1999.

Lieutenant General Whitcomb (*left*) and Major General Nasser Hamad al-Farsi (*right*) shaking hands during the closing ceremony of Camp Doha. The United States has been instrumental in the modernization of the Kuwaiti military.

From the word *diwan*, Arabic for a reception room, we get the word *divan*, a low bed or couch. This is because these rooms were traditionally furnished with mattresses and cushions so that many people could lounge on the floor.

Kuwaiti foreign affairs minister Sheikh Mohammed Sabah al-Salem al-Sabah (*in center*).

FOREIGN RELATIONS

Since the end of the Gulf War in 1991, Kuwait has sought to make allies throughout the world, particularly United Nations Security Council members. In addition to the United States, Kuwait has agreed to defense arrangements with the United Kingdom, Russia, and France. Kuwait has also maintained close ties to other key Arab members of the Gulf War coalition, Egypt and Syria.

Since the U.S.-led invasion of Iraq in 2003, Kuwait has taken a strongly pro-U.S. stance. As the launch pad for the invasion, Kuwait is still home to a large U.S. military presence as part of the U.S. Army's campaign to maintain stability in Iraq.

DIWANIYAH: A FORM OF DEMOCRACY?

In addition to its elected National Assembly, Kuwait has a traditional institution, the *diwaniyah* (dee-WAHN-ee-yah), which allows Kuwaiti men and, sometimes, women to debate and discuss their opinions and to channel these views to their rulers. When Kuwait was a small city-state, this system

AN INDIRECT BUT EFFICIENT ROUTE

An example of the efficient but complex working of the diwaniyah *network might be that of a Kuwaiti boss who finds that his construction business is badly affected by a shortage of Asian workers because of government restrictions on the numbers admitted into Kuwait. He expresses his problems at a family* diwaniyah. *His cousin, who works in the Ministry of Defense, agrees with him. At a* diwaniyah *of army officers and their friends, which he regularly attends, he raises this concern. A fellow guest, who is the husband of the sister of a cabinet minister, then agrees to raise the matter at his family* diwaniyah. *Thus the matter is brought to the attention of a cabinet minister, who might then discuss it with his colleagues. If several of them have also heard of this problem, they will formulate a policy to deal with it.*

ensured that Kuwait was a fairly democratic society where most people could express their views.

Traditionally the *diwaniyah* is a social gathering for men, usually held in a special reception room, also called a *diwaniyah*. These meetings are usually held weekly and are attended, by invitation, by groups of friends and relatives who discuss business and politics over coffee or maybe a meal. They are an occasion for many social and business activities and are also a way of establishing contact with people who can carry participants' concerns and opinions to the ears of the cabinet members, or even to the emir himself.

Most people attend several *diwaniyahs*, meeting different groups of people. In this way common concerns will be discussed and conveyed to the highest *diwaniyahs*. When the National Assembly was closed, the emir encouraged the *diwaniyah* network as an alternative to elected assemblies. The network fueled the pro-democracy movement in Kuwait and was instrumental in the resistance to the Iraqi occupation.

The *diwaniyah* system works well for male Kuwaiti citizens who are admitted to this network. Women have their own more informal visiting networks. They may also express some opinions through their male relatives, who might raise their concerns in male *diwaniyahs*. Non-Kuwaitis may have their own networks, but these are unlikely to overlap with those of Kuwaitis.

ECONOMY

Workers changing pipes on an oil drilling rig.
Oil constitutes a major part of Kuwait's revenue.

T HE ECONOMY OF KUWAIT SHARES a great similarity with those of the country's neighbors. The economies of the Gulf region are distinct from those of both poorer countries and industrialized countries with which they share a similar or higher standard of living. A per capita income of $24,040 conceals serious inequalities between Kuwaitis and expatriates, both in income and in the form of welfare benefits given to all Kuwaitis.

The first and most obvious distinction is the economy's heavy dependence on a single product, petroleum. A second distinctive feature of Kuwait's economy is that income from the export of oil is paid directly to the government. The Kuwaiti government, therefore, has to manage this income within the domestic economy. A third way in which oil-exporting countries such as Kuwait are unique is that most state income is earned in foreign exchange, which can be put only to certain uses.

Right: A shopkeeper stands before his wares in a market.

Most oil economies in the Gulf tend to suffer from a condition called Dutch disease. This occurs when the economy outside the oil sector is undermined by the easy living gained from oil exports. The term stems from the problems faced by the Dutch economy when natural gas was discovered and exploited by the Netherlands for the first time. Welfare provisions grew, and government employment expanded unnecessarily as the state controlled the oil income. Establishing alternative ways of earning money was neglected.

TOO RICH TOO FAST?

Kuwait has few natural resources other than oil. In 2007 Kuwait was estimated to have 101.5 billion barrels, or 8 percent of the world's oil reserves. This makes Kuwait the third-largest producer of oil in the Middle East and the fourth-largest in the world.

Kuwait is the third richest country in the Muslim world. Like its neighbors, the country has been unable to determine how best to spend its oil income. It has spent a good deal of its revenues quite successfully on infrastructure and on health, education, and other services. To be used effectively, imported goods and services require a skilled local labor force, able management, and a strong commercial structure. Kuwait's excess of foreign exchange has resulted in the development of a "slave" economy, in which many goods and services, together with the labor to run them, are imported. Kuwait depends heavily on foreign laborers who often work in poor conditions (although not as bad as in Dubai). But although paid poorly, they choose to work in Kuwait because conditions in their home countries are even worse. Meanwhile Kuwaitis live like masters without serious productive employment. Before 1990 more than 75 percent of the Kuwaiti labor force were foreign nationals. Today the figure is closer to 80 percent, the influx of foreign workers fueled by the high oil prices of recent years. The labor force was estimated to be 2.09 million in 2007.

Per capita income represented by the value of oil exports divided by the number of citizens is extremely high. Generally a low-quality labor force that demands high income, as is the case among Kuwaiti citizens, is a poor basis for establishing competitive agriculture or industry. In short, Kuwaitis will not work for less money than they can receive from the government simply

Oil was discovered in Kuwait in 1938, but the first exports were not made until 1946. Kuwait benefited from the closure of the Iranian oil fields during a period of political unrest in 1951, as well as from the discovery of new oil fields at Mina al-Ahmadi. By 1953 Kuwait had the largest output of all the countries in the Gulf area. Its production was not overtaken by any of its neighbors until 1965.

Kuwait has followed a policy of extracting, refining, and retailing oil. This means it is able to sell higher-priced products rather than lower-priced crude oil. By the mid-1980s, 80 percent of Kuwait's crude oil was refined locally, and 250,000 barrels per day of refined oil were sold as gasoline from 4,400 Kuwaiti-owned gas stations in Europe, under the Q8 logo. Today there remain hundreds of Q8 gas stations in Belgium, the Netherlands, and Sweden. Kuwait has its own tanker fleet to export the oil. It is also involved in the extraction and refining of oil in other countries and has a well-developed petrochemical industry that uses oil by-products.

by being citizens. Producing things in Kuwait would be expensive, as the wages for Kuwaitis would be too high. Apart from very expensive items such as jewelry or bulky items such as furniture, it is cheaper to import most goods from countries where the wages are lower.

WHAT IF THE OIL RUNS OUT?

Oil is a limited product, as is the gas that accompanies it. Kuwait has an estimated 101.5 billion barrels of oil left, which at the current rates of extraction will last for more than 100 years. Only Saudi Arabia and possibly Iraq have greater reserves. Nevertheless the Kuwaiti government has long been aware that future generations of Kuwaitis will not be able to rely on a massive oil income. With this in mind the government embarked on an ambitious policy to protect Kuwait's future by creating a government-run investment body called the Kuwait Investment Authority.

Kuwait decided in the mid-1970s not to attempt to diversify its economy but to concentrate instead on refining and exploration techniques. Oil

Oil is very easy to extract in Kuwait: It is under such natural pressure that it comes spouting out of the ground. Most oil wells in Kuwait are sited on a slight incline so that the oil can easily be moved by gravity through pipes to the coast, where it is refined.

The Kuwaiti government is taking steps to diversify its economy to reduce its dependency on oil for revenue.

production was kept low to maintain output, and financial resources were invested abroad for future generations. Only 10 percent of Kuwaiti oil is used within the country, as it is considered too valuable to burn. The laws to protect Kuwait's future generations oblige the government to invest 10 percent of oil revenues through the Future Generation Fund (FGF) in long-term investments, mostly abroad. These investments account for half of the total revenue generated in Kuwait. Nearly 70 percent of this income is not spent but reinvested. Daily income from these investments is currently about $20 million. No assets can be withdrawn from the FGF unless sanctioned by law. The government owns many commercial ventures around the world, including leisure facilities in the United States such as the Phoenician Resort Hotel in Scottsdale, Arizona. Kuwait has substantial holdings in most of the New York Stock Exchange's leading 100 corporations, as well as in most European countries and in the emerging markets of East Asia.

The government wants to decrease Kuwait's dependence on oil by transforming it into a regional trading and tourism hub. The planned $77 billion Madinat al-Hareer (City of Silk) is the largest real estate development project in the Middle East. The development will include the Burj Mubarak al-Kabir, the world's tallest structure; a desert nature reserve of 0.8 square miles (2 square km); a large business center; environmental areas; sports areas; and tourist attractions, such as hotels, spas, and public gardens. The project was approved in 2008 by the Kuwaiti government, and it is expected to take up to 25 years for completion.

Thanks to these extensive investments outside the Middle East, the Kuwaiti government was able to function, without resorting to borrowing, during the Iraqi invasion and the time that it took to restart oil production.

A RENTIER ECONOMY

Economists and political scientists call oil economies like Kuwait's rentier economies. In a rentier economy, the source of income, or rent, is externally generated, involves little contact with the local economy, goes directly to the state, and is very large.

In Kuwait, revenues have historically come from foreign oil companies. The oil industry creates few related industries, generates money rather than jobs, and is capital intensive—it uses money rather than people.

Revenues from oil go to the state, unlike in most other countries where income from foreign trade goes to the companies that make and export goods. Before oil was discovered, the sheikhs collected taxes on pearling and trading boats.

The state owns the land where oil is found or the rights to exploit it, so it also owns the income from oil. Kuwait's oil revenues account for nearly half of its gross domestic product (GDP), 90 percent of its export revenues, and 5 percent of its government income.

ORGANIZATION OF PETROLEUM EXPORTING COUNTRIES

OPEC was established in 1960 by five oil-producing countries—Iraq, Iran, Venezuela, Saudi Arabia, and Kuwait—as a reaction to the policies of the large international oil companies, which controlled prices and kept most of the profits. These five countries were producing 85 percent of the world's oil. OPEC aimed to raise international oil prices and increase the share of the profits that the producing states received. OPEC's membership grew to 13 countries, which included most of the Arab Gulf states. Kuwait later also joined the Organization of Arab Petroleum Exporting Countries (OAPEC), which had a more political agenda. In the 1970s OAPEC boycotted Israel and its supporting countries and raised oil prices by 70 percent, causing a world oil crisis. OPEC and OAPEC have allowed countries such as Kuwait to bargain for favorable oil prices and to agree on production levels to maintain those prices. The Iraqi invasion of Kuwait illustrated that not all of the members agreed on production levels and prices.

Kuwait's oil production in 1972 reached 3.3 million barrels of oil a day, which was gradually reduced to around 1 million barrels a day before the 1990 Iraqi invasion. This was a result of both lower world demand due to energy conservation and Kuwait's desire to conserve its supplies. This meant a decrease of 66 percent in oil revenues over 18 years, which was offset by Kuwait's overseas investments. Kuwait previously produced 2.7 million barrels of oil a day, and has now increased production by 300,000 barrels per day.

THE EFFECTS OF OIL DEPENDENCY

Kuwait's rentier economy has affected the nature of the Kuwaiti state. A rentier state has a different function from that of other states. In most countries the government collects taxes for redistribution. In Kuwait there are few taxes, and the government simply distributes oil revenues through direct transfers, social services, and state jobs. The country has no Internal Revenue Service, but it does have ministries for health, social affairs, and education. It also has a large ministry for oil. The Kuwaiti government can distribute revenue, but it cannot redistribute wealth—that is, it can give to the poor, but it cannot take from the rich. This means that the state has limited economic policy tools and little flexibility.

A vendor selling produce along the street. Kuwait has to import a large proportion of its food.

As in other rentier economies, oil weakened certain old classes in Kuwait, such as the merchants, because the state no longer needed their taxes, and Kuwaitis no longer depended on them for employment. If oil wealth destroyed certain social groups, it also created a new one: a huge class of civil servants and bureaucrats who depend on the state for their existence.

In Kuwait the state was initially stable as it created a new social structure. But with no taxation the government does not need to consider the wishes of the people, because their money is not being spent. Being wealthy also means the government is able to buy the support of some people. Kuwaitis have recently shown, however, that they are no longer content simply being wealthy but want more say in shaping the country.

Another drawback of a rentier economy is that it is dependent on the outside world. Kuwait relies on other countries for food, water, and most of its consumer goods and raw materials. It must rely on foreign markets and the price they are prepared to pay for oil; it also relies on foreign labor and imported goods.

AN OUTWARD-FACING ECONOMY

With agriculture never a successful pursuit because of the harsh climate, Kuwaitis have traditionally looked elsewhere for food and even water. In the past water was imported from Iraq. Long-distance trade and pearling were, until the 1930s, the heart of the economy.

Before oil, Kuwait's economy depended on the movements of the bedouin and caravans from Baghdad and Aleppo, on the vagaries of Indian and African markets, and on the pearl-buying patterns of wealthy Europeans. With oil this pattern of dependency has deepened. It is cheaper now to import most goods, and as Kuwait is accessible only by air or sea, this means supplies are at the mercy of external events. During the Iran-Iraq War supplies coming in by ship became unreliable, and this affected the availability and prices of consumer goods.

A dhow laden with cargo. Boatbuilding was once a significant part of Kuwait's economy.

THE WORLD OF WORK

According to statistics from Kuwait's General Secretariat of Planning and Development, the number of Kuwaitis working in the private sector is about 44,000, compared with the 311,000 Kuwaitis in government employment. Employment in Kuwait generally falls into three categories: the government sector (ministries, other public authorities, and the state-owned oil companies), the private sector, and domestic service. About 80 percent of the Kuwaitis in the workforce are employed in the government sector, as every Kuwaiti citizen is guaranteed a job for life. Salaries are high, and Kuwaitis do not like to work for private companies unless they are owned by their families. The labor force in Kuwait numbered 2,093,000 in 2007,

The Kuwaiti government has introduced legislation to try to get more private companies in Kuwait to hire Kuwaitis. The idea is to make Kuwaitis less dependent on the government for employment as well as to expose Kuwaitis to the world of international commerce. The government has forced all companies, by sector, to keep a fixed percentage of their employees as locals. To make this more attractive to private businesses, the government also pays a fixed amount of the salary to the employee.

an increase of 6.7 percent from the previous year. This was mainly due to an influx of foreign workers, who make up more than 80 percent of the workforce in the private sector. In 2009, it was reported that the number of expatriate workers in Kuwait fell from 1.77 million (2007) to 1.75 million (2008). This drop can be attributed to an economic slowdown, which led several companies to retrench some of their foreign employees. The majority of non-Kuwaitis work in the private or business sector or as domestic servants.

From 2007 to 2008, there was an increase in the proportion of Kuwaitis in the workforce from 324,000 to 336,000—an increase of about 3.4 percent. Most Kuwaitis hold jobs in the public sector.

Office hours are quite short in the government sector, and this allows many Kuwaitis to have an additional private business in the afternoon. In the private sector there is a long afternoon break; this, together with an early start, is because of the hot weather. Because of air-conditioning this is gradually being phased out for a regular working day.

During the fasting month of Ramadan, hours are altered. Generally ministries and oil companies work from 7:00 A.M. to 2:00 P.M., while many other companies are open from 8:00 A.M. to 1:00 P.M., and then again from 4:30 P.M. to 7:00 P.M. Banks are open from 7:30 A.M. to 2:30 P.M.

Most workers in the private sector, like this gold craftsman, are non-Kuwaitis.

Kuwaitis checking out cars in a showroom. Automobiles are one of the main imports of the oil-rich state.

TRADING TRADITIONS

Today the majority of Kuwaitis work for the government, largely providing domestic services in local education, health care, and oil-related industries. Although oil makes up 90 percent of exports, which are all in government hands, more than $6 billion worth of imports arrive in Kuwait every year. Many of these are arranged by Kuwaiti or expatriate traders. Other than oil very little is produced in Kuwait, but Kuwaitis are demanding and discerning consumers. As there are no sales taxes and few import duties, goods can be sold in large volumes at reasonable prices. The main sources of imports are the United States (12.9 percent), Japan (8.7 percent), Germany (7.5 percent), China (7.1 percent), Saudi Arabia (6.4 percent), Italy, Britain, India, and South Korea. Imports include food, automobiles, building materials, machinery, and textiles. Kuwaitis are keen on the latest technology, and all Kuwaitis have cell telephones, the latest televisions, and computers.

> ## DOMESTIC WORKERS

Among the many foreign workers in Kuwait are hundreds of thousands of domestic servants, mainly from India, Sri Lanka, and the Philippines. Precise figures of the number of domestic workers are hard to confirm, but some estimates suggest there is one domestic servant for every two Kuwaitis. Most are young Asian women employed by families to cook meals, clean the home, and look after the children. In the past the working conditions and salary levels were not regulated by the government. Some domestic servants complained of abuse by employers, which included not being allowed a day off, working up to 15 hours a day, and not being paid on time. Some complained of being beaten, locked in their rooms, and refused permission to go outside the home. A standardized contract for foreign domestic workers introduced in October 2006 led to some improvements, but abuses still persist.

TRANSPORTATION

There are seven airports in the country, of which four have paved runways. Kuwait International Airport serves as the principal hub for international air travel. Internal air travel is not necessary, although helicopters are used by companies and some individuals. Public transportation is limited to taxis and some buses. Kuwait has no railway, although one is planned for along the coastal corridor. Also in the works are a bus service to link the new towns and passenger ferries for the islands.

Increased security during the Iraqi war led to huge traffic congestion.

More than 1 million motor vehicles are registered in Kuwait, or one vehicle for every 2.5 residents. Kuwait has a poor road safety record: In 2006 the government reported 60,410 vehicle accidents, with 460 deaths and 9,100 serious injuries. The government has attempted to crack down on dangerous driving by introducing radar surveillance and threatening drivers who run a red light with imprisonment, but this has had only limited effect.

ENVIRONMENT

Flamingos in Kuwait Bay at Sulaibikhat at sunset.

CHAPTER 5

KUWAIT HAS A HARSH, ARID climate, with scarce water resources and poor soil. In such a climate, the main environmental concerns are water shortages, desertification (the turning of fertile land into desert), and the pollution of the marine and coastal environment, especially after damage caused by the Iraqi occupation in 1990—91.

The government of Kuwait supports a number of organizations in protecting and preserving the local environment. These include the Environment Public Authority (EPA), which was established in October 1996. The EPA is mainly concerned with preserving natural resources, although it also monitors the state and quality of air, water, and soil. Kuwait is a member of the Regional Organization for the Protection of the Marine Environment, which has its headquarters in Kuwait City. Along with other countries in the Gulf, each year on April 24 Kuwait observes Regional Environment Day. Public projects in schools and government departments try to raise awareness of the threats to the local marine and land environments.

Right: A road in Kuwait. The natural environment in Kuwait is very harsh.

Water towers located in Kuwait City ensure that the nation collects as much water as it can.

WATER RESOURCES

As a small desert country with little rainfall, Kuwait has extremely limited freshwater. In the past Kuwait spent large sums of money trying to find local underground water, but with little success. Until the 1950s all drinking water was transported to Kuwait by boat. However, Kuwait's oil wealth has allowed it to develop some of the world's largest and most modern desalination facilities. Desalination is a method whereby salt water is treated to remove excess salt so that the water can be used for drinking, cleaning, watering crops, and other activities. Desalination is an expensive process and much more costly than taking water from rivers or underground. Desalination plants provide most of the sanitary and drinking water in Kuwait today.

Most of Kuwait's water is desalinated through a method called multistage flash distillation. Seawater is distilled by converting a portion of the water into steam in a series of stages. The steam is then converted back into water that can be used for irrigation, drinking, and cleaning. In 2008 the Ministry of Electricity and Water of Kuwait awarded the U.S. company Doosan Heavy Industries and Construction the contract to construct the Shuwaikh Seawater Reverse Osmosis (SWRO) Desalination Plant. Using a new type of technology, this plant will supply drinking water for 450,000 residents in Kuwait City.

DESERTIFICATION

Desertification—the turning of fertile land into desert—is a serious problem in Kuwait. Desertification has been caused by the development of the oil industry, the expansion of cities, water and wind erosion, and the damage caused by the Iraqi occupation and other wars in the Gulf region. Natural vegetation has deteriorated to the point where it covers less than 10 percent of the country and is decreasing at a rate of 110 square miles (285 square km) each year.

An increasing proportion of arable Kuwaiti land is being turned into desert.

The government has made several attempts to combat desertification. It has carried out the mass planting of local flora as well as planted exotic, ornamental plants that can endure harsh climatic conditions. The government has also sponsored studies of the soil and climate to determine which plants are best suited to the harsh, dry conditions so that these plants can be nurtured.

AIR POLLUTION—WHERE CAR IS KING

Along with its Gulf neighbors and the United States, Kuwait is considered among the most carbon-polluting countries in the world, partly because of its oil-producing activities but primarily because of the huge number of vehicles per capita. Low fuel costs and a high level of earnings have created conditions where there are more than a million vehicles on Kuwait's roads—one vehicle for every 2.5 residents—which create 97,795 tons (99,364 metric tons) of carbon emissions each year, or 0.4 percent of the world's total carbon emissions.

Vehicle emissions contribute to a large part of Kuwait's air pollution.

DAMAGE DURING THE IRAQI OCCUPATION

The Iraqi occupation forces caused environmental damage on an unprecedented scale. Three days into the war, Iraqi troops opened the valves on the Mina al-Ahmadi Sea Island Terminal, releasing millions of gallons of oil into the waters of the Gulf. Estimates vary, but it is thought that 6-8 million barrels of crude oil were spilled into the marine environment. The resulting oil slick was more than 100 miles (161 km) long and 40 miles (64 km) wide. At least 286 miles (460 km) of coastline, most of it in Saudi Arabia and Bahrain, were affected, devastating coastal wildlife and destroying large areas of mangroves. Migratory birds, cormorants, dolphins, and turtles were all heavily affected. The corals that form the base of the ecosystem of the warm shallow Gulf were poisoned by oil. With the corals damaged or destroyed, many of the creatures that lived off them also died. Many birds died because they drank from the oil spills thinking they were water. The slick was fought by crews from international oil companies, and eventually around a million barrels of crude oil were recovered from the slick.

The retreating Iraqi army set fire to nearly 600 oil wells—almost two-thirds of the wells in the country—and the fires were not fully extinguished until November 1991, eight months after the end of the war. With at least 2 million barrels of oil lost each day, this was an environmental disaster of catastrophic proportions. Experts calculated that this waste increased world oil consumption by 5 percent and the worldwide output of carbon dioxide by about 2 percent for as long as it was allowed to continue. After eight months of intensive work, international firefighting crews put out the fires, at a cost of $1.5 billion to Kuwait.

The burning of the oil wells dramatically affected air quality, releasing 2 million tons (2.03 million metric tons) of carbon dioxide into the atmosphere and creating a cloud that blocked out the sun for many days. The toxic air caused breathing problems among many Kuwaitis, and people throughout the Gulf region developed asthma. Smoke from the Kuwait oil fires also dramatically altered weather patterns throughout the Middle East during 1991: Lower atmospheric wind blew the smoke along the eastern half of the Arabian Peninsula, and cities such as Dhahran, Riyadh, and Bahrain experienced days of smoke-covered skies and harmful carbon fallout.

The sabotage of the oil wells also damaged the desert environment. Unlit oil from the wells formed about 300 oil lakes that contaminated around 40 million tons

(40.6 million metric tons) of sand and earth. The oil lakes evaporated to create toxins that poisoned the air and damaged the health of both humans and animals. Intensive cleaning by the Kuwaiti authorities meant much of the oil was cleared by 1995, but the dry climate also partially solidified some of the lakes. Over time the oil has continued to sink into the sand. In recent years experts have, through various processes of composting and venting (airing), turned the oil lakes into soil of such a good quality that it could be used to create landscape gardens. The creation of the Japanese Garden in al-Ahmadi offers hope that other oil damages can also be made biologically useful.

PLANT LIFE

Less than 0.5 percent of Kuwait is forested. The little forest that does exist has remained stable in recent years. During the 10-year period from 1990 to 2000, Kuwait gained an average of 494 acres (200 ha) of forest per year, or an increase of 6.6 percent per year. Between 2000 and 2005, the amount of forest decreased by 4 percent a year. This means that between 1990 and 2005, Kuwait's forests remained at a constant level, at around 7,413 acres (3,000 ha), neither increasing nor shrinking.

Kuwait is home to 400 species of plants, the most common of which are bright green rimth and red-flowered al-awsaj, both of which are popular grazing plants for camels. During winter there is a remarkable amount of plant life in Kuwait, enough to provide food for local camel herds. Unfortunately overgrazing by goats and sheep is damaging the desert's natural plant life.

ANIMAL LIFE AND ENDANGERED SPECIES

There are 25 mammal species native to Kuwait. According to the International Union for Conservation of Nature, none are critically endangered, one is endangered, four are vulnerable, and one is near threatened. The dugong—from the order Sirenia—is the only animal considered endangered in the Gulf

Kuwait was thoroughly cleaned up after the war damage of the Iraqi occupation, and today Kuwaitis can enjoy camping in the desert without fear of coming across unexploded bombs and other military refuse.

region. Dugongs are plant-eating mammals that inhabit rivers, estuaries, coastal waters, swamps, and coastal wetlands. They are totally aquatic, in that they never leave the water, even to give birth. The Euphrates jerboa, a type of rodent that can be found throughout the Gulf region, is considered vulnerable, with its natural habitat—the desert—being increasingly encroached upon by expanding towns and the building of roads and other infrastructure.

It is estimated that 16 species of bird breeds are indigenous to Kuwait, the most common of which is the desert lark. Because Kuwait lies at the crossroads of several important migratory routes, the total bird count for the country is around 280 species. Inland birds of prey such as the kestrel and the short-toed eagle can be seen hunting for big-eared fennecs and the ever-present jerboas. Common lizards include dhoubs (a type of monitor lizard), and dung beetles and scorpions can be seen everywhere. Each April the globally threatened lesser kestrel (*Falco naumanni*) can be seen passing over Kuwait City.

To the north of Kuwait Bay, the cliffs of Jal Az-Zor Ridge are home for many migratory falcons that perch along the ridge in the early morning. The region, which includes a ridge and coastal sand dunes, salt marshes, and mudflats,

The dugong is an mammal that spends all of its time in the water.

A falcon with its handler.

has been turned into a protected area known as Jal Az-Zor National Park. The migrating black vulture passes through this area in March and October, while the imperial eagle, as well as the lesser kestrel, can be seen in March and October/November.

The reed-lined pools of the al-Jahrah wetlands are also a haven for numerous bird species, especially the buzzard, the spotted eagle, the steppe eagle, the imperial eagle, the marsh harrier, the lesser kestrel, and the black vulture.

Pearly goatfish, spiked tripod fish, and silver pomfrets are among the many colorful species of fish caught by fishermen in Kuwait Bay. Crabs and mudskippers are also residents of Kuwait's rich marine environment. All of these fish provide tasty snacks for black-winged stilts, teals, terns, and Socotra cormorants, which also share the coastline. Flamingos are also found in Kuwait Bay.

NATIONAL PARKS

The nature reserve on Bubiyan Island (333 square miles; 863 square km) is one of Kuwait's few national parks. Bubiyan is linked to the mainland by a

1.5-mile (2.4-km) concrete girder bridge over the Khor al-Sabiya Channel; the bridge is used only by the military. Consisting mostly of marshland and creeks, Bubiyan Island is home to wading birds and numerous coastal marine animals. It was heavily mined during the Gulf War.

In 2003 the Jaber al-Kuwait Marine Life Park was opened by the minister of energy, Sheikh Ahmad al-Fahad al-Sabah, during a special underwater ceremony. Accompanied by a group of divers, the minister laid some stone blocks designed to encourage the growth of coral reefs. The Jaber al-Kuwait Marine Life Park, like the 19 other sea reserves already in existence, was set up to encourage marine life back into Kuwaiti waters after the pollution and destruction suffered during the Iraqi occupation of 1990—91.

In 2004 the Sabah al-Ahmad Wildlife Reserve was opened by Sheikh Sabah al-Ahmad al-Sabah, who was the prime minister at the time. The park had been established in the early 1990s as the National Park of Kuwait, near Subayhiyah, in the northeast of the country. Covering 124 square miles (320 square km), the reserve is a sanctuary for flora and fauna and includes a diverse environment encompassing hills, sandy beaches, and muddy coastal waters. The wildlife protected in the reserve includes local rare animals and plants. The Kuwaiti government sees the reserve as an asset for the country's future and encourages young Kuwaitis to volunteer for conservation work within the park.

ECOTOURISM

Roughly 91,000 tourists visit Kuwait each year, which is a very small number compared with many other countries. Most visitors tend to spend their time in Kuwait City in one of the international hotels or perhaps enjoy water sports and beach life in one of the luxury coastal resorts. A small number do venture into the desert, however, where the ecosystem is fragile. Car tracks can scar desert rocks and damage plants, insects, and other animals. Trash does not biodegrade as it would in a wetter climate, and even small amounts can leave a trace for decades. Local campers have also been known to discard trash in the desert.

Among the most dangerous snakes in Kuwait is the black desert cobra. This snake has an extremely toxic venom. However, it is a species very rarely seen by humans. In bedouin folklore the snake is held to be so dangerous that if it is killed, its spirit will return to destroy its attacker!

KUWAITIS

A Kuwaiti man. Most Kuwaitis see themselves as part of the wider Arab community.

CHAPTER 6

KUWAIT IS A GULF ARAB SOCIETY. Kuwaitis identify themselves as Arabs from Kuwait, and they feel a part of the wider Arab world. Kuwait has a common identity with other Gulf Arab nations and shares cultural traits with Bahrain, Oman, Qatar, the United Arab Emirates, Saudi Arabia, and Iraq.

Gulf Arab culture is a mixture of Islamic and Arab culture, with African, Indian, and Persian influences. Kuwait itself has a distinct identity, forged by the experience of migration and building the Kuwaiti settlement. More recently the Iraqi invasion helped shape this distinctness.

Kuwaiti society, like many other societies, is divided by class, wealth, tribal affiliations, religion, and aspirations. Although the majority of Kuwaitis are descendants of the Bani Utub families who founded Kuwait, some are of other tribal origins or from other Gulf states or Iran. The reliance on expatriate workers has led to Kuwaiti citizens becoming a minority, and this has created serious social problems. According to the 2008 figures, the population stands at approximately 2,596,799. This is an increase of 6.8 percent from the previous year.

Right: Kuwaitis possess a distinct identity, shaped by their shared experiences of early and recent history.

Kuwaitis have a strong sense of identity and community, considering themselves part of the wider Arab world. Equally important are family ties, and much of what they do is in a bid to foster these ties.

Bedouin children outside a tent at a bedouin camp. Many bedouins are not considered legal residents of Kuwait.

KUWAITIS IN THE MINORITY

In Kuwait non-Arabs
are described
as *ajams*.
Traditionally
ajam referred
to people of
Persian ancestry.
This community
expanded in the
early 1900s after
the fall of the
Persian Empire.
The Persian
population in
Kuwait has
been declining,
however, due to
low birthrates and
intermarriage.

Most of the people who live in Kuwait are not Kuwaitis but foreign workers, mostly from Asia and other Arab countries. In 1957 non-Kuwaitis already made up 45 percent of the population. Before the Iraqi invasion, they formed up to 75 percent of the population and more than 80 percent of the workforce. Slightly more than half of these were Asians; the rest were mostly Arabs, primarily Palestinians, Jordanians, and Egyptians. Palestinians were particularly evident in managerial jobs. In 2003 more than 400,000 Indians lived in Kuwait, making them the largest expatriate community. After Kuwait was liberated from the Iraqi occupation, nearly 400,000 Palestinians living in Kuwait were expelled because of their government's open support for the Iraqi forces. Today only a few thousand Palestinians remain.

The presence of so many foreigners in the country has been a source of anxiety for Kuwaitis, who fear that their culture will be overwhelmed. More than 120 nationalities live in Kuwait, and adherents of almost all religions can be found.

After the Gulf War, attempts were made to reduce the number of foreigners, often by deporting them. Many workers who tried to return from their home countries were denied entry. Kuwait's people break down into the following broad ethnic groups: Kuwaitis, other Arab peoples, Asians (primarily Bangladeshis, Pakistanis, Indians, Sri Lankans, and Filipinos), and stateless Arabs, or *bidoons* (be-DOONS).

CITIZENS WITHOUT CITIZENSHIP?

Foreigners who live in Kuwait will never receive the equivalent of a green card or Kuwaiti citizenship, but this also applies to many people who would appear to be Kuwaitis. Once Kuwait became independent, citizenship became dependent on proven Kuwaiti ancestry, with family residence from at least 1920. This was difficult to prove, especially for nomadic tribes, many of whom had not seen the importance of citizenship

The majority of Kuwait's population are foreigners.

when they had had no need of the state. First-class citizenship was given to a third of the native population, another third were given partial or second-class citizenship, and the remaining third were considered potential citizens—*bidoons jinsiya*—or *bidoons*. Citizens and other inhabitants were clearly separated in all respects, legally and socially. Government payments were restricted to citizens only, but in many other respects, the *bidoons* were treated as citizens and hoped to be recognized as such one day.

Historically many bedouin tribes lived on the outskirts of Kuwait City and in the desert beyond. Often they served as armed retainers to the ruling al-Sabah family. After independence some bedouin were offered citizenship in return for military service and support in the National Assembly. Some collected passports from more than one Gulf state, but others became stateless, or *bidoons*. Many of these stateless bedouin lived in the desert in or near Kuwait but had no documentary proof of their residence.

SOCIAL DIVISIONS

In Kuwait divisions exist between the very rich and the less rich; there are very few poor Kuwaiti citizens. There is a social division between the Bani Utub, the merchant families who are descendants of the founders of Kuwait and who include the ruling family, and the rest of the citizenry. Of the latter one of the biggest distinct social groups is the bedouin, many of whom are *bidoons*.

The ruling al-Sabah family became economically superior after the oil boom; as political rulers, they controlled the revenue. All al-Sabah family

A cloth merchant. The merchant class has survived many economic and social changes brought about by oil wealth.

Kuwait is a predominantly Muslim nation, but allows for religious freedom.

members receive a monthly check from the civil list. They marry within the family and hold key positions in the government, as well as in most business, educational, and other ventures. In many respects they are above the law, as any complaints against them are not dealt with by ordinary courts but by family councils.

The oil boom changed the class structure dramatically. Kuwait's rentier economy makes access to the state, rather than access to private property, the prime determinant of wealth. Classes such as artisans and those who worked for traders opted for jobs with the state, taking on new identities as bureaucrats and technocrats.

Nevertheless the merchant class did not disappear. This was because the merchants had established their own culture and interests, with social institutions such as *diwaniyahs* (social and political gatherings) and marriages between the families. The government found it cheaper and easier to buy their support than to remove them, so the merchant class remained intact as a group.

RELIGIOUS DIVISIONS

The constitution of Kuwait recognizes religious freedom, although it forbids attempts to convert Muslims to other religions. The small, mostly expatriate,

A section in the souk where clothes are sold.

Christian and Hindu communities can practice their faiths freely and have their own places of worship. There is also a small Jewish community of merchant families.

Eight-five percent of the population is Muslim. The majority of Kuwaitis are Sunni Muslims, but up to 30 percent are Shiite Muslims. The Shiite community is diverse and consists of Gulf Arabs who emigrated from Bahrain and Saudi Arabia with short stays in Iran, and Persian Shiites whose ancestors spoke Persian and who maintain ties to Iran. As they often marry within their own communities, they each have a distinct identity, although they also have a strong Kuwaiti identity.

The Iranian revolution encouraged some Shiites to complain of unfair treatment in Kuwait by the Sunni majority. This led to the government introducing more discriminatory measures against them, alienating loyal Shiites. During the Iraqi occupation many Shiites remained in Kuwait, because they felt unwelcome in Saudi Arabia, a conservative Sunni society. Shiites are regarded with suspicion by the government.

TRADITIONAL CLOTHES

In Kuwait traditional Arab clothes are worn alongside European-style suits and dresses, casual clothes, Indian saris, and Punjabi suits. Although some Kuwaitis once felt that European clothes were stylish and better than traditional wear, they now feel proud of their cultural heritage and realize that their clothes are not only attractive but also practical for the local weather and lifestyle.

Although special sections of the souk (market) sell ready-made, traditional clothes, often imported from the Far East, the discerning Kuwaiti will choose the material to have his or her clothes made by a tailor. Many Indian and Pakistani tailors specialize in traditional Kuwaiti clothes, which are custom-made at a low price.

WOMEN'S CLOTHES Glancing at Kuwaiti women in the street will show two types of clothing. Many professional or young women wear European clothes, but some will wear a large headscarf, called a *hijab*, to cover their hair and neck. Other women wear a black *abaya*, a sort of cloak that covers the body and clothes in loose folds. Most bedouin and older women cover their faces with a black cloth, or *bushiya* (boosh-ee-YAH), or wear a burka, which covers both the face and the body.

A mix of traditional and contemporary styles of dressing.

The most common form of traditional woman's dress is the *thob* (thohb), a long, loose dress. These can be made in any color or fabric and are often lavishly embroidered with jewels, sequins, and gold thread. They may be made of transparent material and worn over another dress and trousers. If Kuwaiti women wear European clothes to work or outside the house, they will almost always wear a *dara'a* (dah-RAH-ah), a simple form of the *thob* like a housecoat, once they get home. Many women wear European-style clothes that are made with floor-length skirts, always with long sleeves and worn with the hijab. They may wear smarter versions of the *dara'a* to work or outside the house.

Kuwaiti women take great care with their appearance and tend to wear elaborate makeup, jewelry, and hairstyles. Most use black eyeliner for their dark eyes, the way generations of Kuwaiti women have done before them. French perfumes waft through all the social gatherings, and most women visit beauty parlors and spend hours at beauty treatments.

WOMEN'S DRESS: A PRIVATE CHOICE? The Islamic way of dressing for women was, until recently, considered a matter of private choice in Kuwait. But lately it has become more of a public issue, particularly at Kuwait University. The Islamist opposition wants Islamic dress made compulsory, but others want it banned from the university and public offices. During the occupation by Iraq some exiled Kuwaitis were influenced by contact with the conservative Saudi Arabians, while others were influenced by Westerners. Their experiences resulted in various views about women, particularly about their clothes.

Women wearing face coverings have been officially banned from driving for safety reasons, but they can still be seen behind the wheel. Some women feel that the Islamist groups offer the only opposition to the government and show their support by wearing traditional clothes. Some women who were brave enough to wear European clothes in the past now feel they should wear them with long hemlines, or they now opt for traditional clothes.

MEN'S CLOTHES The traditional clothes still favored by Kuwaiti men are very similar to those of merchants of the 19th century. They consist of a dishdasha, or long robe, worn over long, white trousers, or *sirwal* (seer-WAHL). A scarf, or *gatra* (GAT-rah), is worn on the head, held in place by a decorative rope, or *agal*. In summer the dishdasha and the *gatra* are sparkling white, but in winter, black, navy, beige, gray, or even blue woolen dishdashas are worn, and the white *gatra* may be replaced with a red-and-white checkered one. A loose, long coat called a *bisht* (beesht) may also be worn, usually in sober colors. A fur-lined coat, or *farwah* (fahr-WAH), is also worn in winter by bedouin, who spend cold nights out in the desert.

Most Kuwaiti men wear traditional clothes all the time, at least while in Kuwait, and all wear casual versions of traditional clothes at home. It is easy to tell the non-Kuwaiti Arabs, such as the Palestinians, as they wear European clothes to work, keeping traditional clothes for the home. Kuwaiti men also carry worry beads, or *masabah* (mas-AB-bah). Rarely is a Kuwaiti man seen without a set of beads, which are rolled, spun around the fingers, or passed from hand to hand.

Professor Faiza al-Kharafi was the president of Kuwait University from 1993 to 2002. A professor of chemistry, she graduated from college in Egypt in 1967, obtaining a PhD in Kuwait and becoming a professor in 1987. She also became the dean of the science faculty. She led Kuwait's sole institution of higher learning, which was established in the year before she graduated, and directed 1,500 employees and more than 17,400 students annually. She is the author of 62 books. In 1995 she was voted the Most Admired Woman of the Decade by the American Bibliographical Institute.

CHILDREN'S CLOTHES Many Kuwaiti children are well dressed in expensive foreign clothes. Most wear fashionable European clothes on a daily basis, and many shops sell imported designer clothes that cost more than they do in London or Paris.

Local tailors do, however, make traditional clothes for children, who often dress just like their parents when they attend social gatherings. The boys will be in dishdashas and the girls will wear *thobs* and maybe even miniature *abayas*. All children attending state schools wear uniforms.

Children wearing Western-style clothes.

Kuwait has a young population, with the average age being 26 years old. About 44 percent are under the age of 15.

LIFESTYLE

Kuwaitis at a market.

CHAPTER 7

I N KUWAIT THE FAMILY IS THE BASIC social unit. At the highest levels the government is based on family ties, and throughout all levels of society, Kuwaiti political, business, and social life continues to revolve around the family.

Although the Kuwaiti government has provided one of the most comprehensive social-welfare programs in the world, Kuwaitis still tend to see the family rather than the state as their main source of support. The importance of the family is enhanced by Kuwait's small size and population, which allows accessibility to political leaders through family networks, by means of the *diwaniyah* meetings.

Kuwaiti men at a traditional tea house. Their short working hours afford them the time to socialize with friends and family.

For the majority of Kuwaiti men, social life revolves around the diwaniyah, *a weekly meeting, generally of men who are related and their friends. Over coffee they discuss business and politics, arrange introductions, or grant favors. Diwaniyahs may be held at any time but tend to be mostly in the afternoon and evening. Tea and other drinks are always served, as well as snacks such as fruits and nuts. A meal may be served, especially late at night, when the guests may bring with them pots of special food. The style of a* diwaniyah *meeting is usually quite traditional. Guests remove their shoes and sit on the floor. If a meal is served it will be spread on a newspaper or a cloth, depending on the degree of formality, and the food eaten from communal dishes. Men may attend several* diwaniyahs *a week, and there may be hundreds of sessions taking place every night in every Kuwaiti suburb. Typically a man will hold a* diwaniyah *on Saturday and Sunday evenings, and his son will host one on Thursday and Friday evenings. The other evenings may be spent at other* diwaniyahs *or with close relatives.*

Despite oil wealth, Western influences, the trauma of the Iraqi invasion, and the impact of the U.S. invasion of Iraq, family values remain conservative, based firmly on Islamic principles. A woman's role in the family as wife and mother, for instance, remains central to her identity despite increased education and participation in the labor force.

Kuwait is a country of very visible wealth and conspicuous consumption. Kuwaitis like to have the newest and best of everything. They also generally have a lot of time on their hands, thanks to the short working hours. Apart from the desert, there is urban life, where everyone drives, or is driven, in their plush air-conditioned cars between air-conditioned houses, shopping malls, and offices. Kuwait is on the whole clean and organized. Few traces of antiquity remain, and these are now carefully preserved.

Roughly 60 percent of the population of Kuwait are males, one of the highest ratios in the world.

A PLACE FOR EVERYONE WITHIN THE FAMILY

If the family is the most important unit in Kuwait, children are the focus of the family. Kuwaitis love children, and they are included in almost all social gatherings. Even when there are servants to care for them, parents will still

A Kuwaiti family enjoying a day out at Kuwait City's water park.

be fully involved in their children's lives. Most forms of entertainment are aimed at families, and there are few social activities that are restricted to adults. The concept of boarding or summer school does not exist in Kuwait. As grandparents may well be part of the family unit, children are generally surrounded by devoted relatives. Some Kuwaitis are concerned about the new generation, as children are usually overindulged, and servants are reluctant to discipline them. Nearly all Kuwaiti families have a live-in foreign "maid" who is responsible for most of the housework and some, sometimes much, of the childrearing.

Children tend to be separated by gender early on, and from the time they are old enough to sit still, boys often attend the *diwaniyahs* with their fathers. Girls stay at home or visit with their mothers, although small girls are welcomed into male gatherings, often with great delight. Children live at home until they marry, and possibly even after that, especially if the parents would otherwise be left alone. Unmarried adults almost never live alone, although they may have separate apartments within a family complex.

Generally in Kuwait one's position in the family depends on gender and age. Men and older people have higher status in the family, and their opinions are the most highly respected. Although the government provides free care for the elderly, it is needed only in the rare cases of old people with no family. Older people live in the family as respected guardians of tradition. It would be a social embarrassment to abandon one's parents. Religious and traditional values ensure that the family provides for all its members.

KUWAITI WOMEN: MANY GAINS, BUT STILL A LONG WAY TO GO

Popular conceptions of the role of women in the Arab Gulf states do not apply in Kuwait. Women are not enslaved in harems, shrouded in black (unless they choose to be), or denied any public role, especially since they have gained the right to vote and stand for public office. Men and women have different identities and interests, however, and men and women are by no means equal. The family is the center of social life, and women's roles within the family are primarily as wives and mothers. The majority of Kuwaiti men and women marry, and usually remarry if they are divorced or widowed. The few unmarried women live with their families.

Kuwaiti family law is largely based on Islamic law, which treats men and women quite differently. Women usually need the permission of a male guardian to marry, and a woman's inheritance is half that of a man's.

Women volunteers helping special-needs children. Kuwaiti women are now better educated and make up the majority of students at Kuwait University.

The government supports equality between the sexes in several areas. Women have ready access to housing, health care, and education. Although the literacy rate for women is lower than that for men (91 percent as opposed to 94 percent), the situation is improving. In 1960 the first group of Kuwaiti women was sent to study at Cairo University in Egypt. Soon after the opening of Kuwait University in 1966, women made up the majority of students (more than 60 percent). Of the students majoring in science, 70 percent are women, although they make up only 34 percent in law and 38 percent in engineering and petroleum. Still this compares favorably with the percentage of women in American universities.

WOMEN AT WORK

Despite the number of women graduates, many of them are unlikely to work. In 1985 only 13.8 percent of Kuwaiti women over the age of 15 worked, but that was nonetheless a significant rise from 1975, when only 6 percent worked. Today 60 percent of Kuwaiti women work, a dramatic increase from the previous decades. One-third of working women are teachers, while the others

Women in Kuwait do not need to work and are encouraged to remain at home.

On May 16, 2005, the National Assembly voted to introduce women's suffrage. In the 2006 election there were more than 340,000 eligible voters, 57 percent of them women.

A Kuwaiti girl in class. Women in Kuwait enjoy favorable employment benefits.

work primarily in the social services and clerical positions, although some are active in the business world. Most of the working women are foreigners. The reason for the low number of working women lies partly within the society's attitude toward work, for both men and women.

In Kuwait fewer people than in any other country need to work for salary. Some older Kuwaitis object to women working, especially when this means they would have to come in contact with men. As women live with their families, they must respect the decision of the head of the household.

Kuwaitis entertain a great deal, have servants to supervise, and have high standards of housework to meet. There are no state nurseries, and in the past foreign nannies were employed. This became a controversial issue, and there was even a campaign against the influence of foreign nannies on children. Now women have up to two years of maternity leave at half pay. The working day for state employees is short, usually ending at 2:00 P.M., so working conditions for Kuwaiti women are very favorable, allowing them to be home in time for lunch with their children. In addition, employers are usually understanding about women needing time off to care for sick children. Nevertheless it appears that just as most Kuwaiti men are ambivalent about work, women are even more so. In 2007 the Kuwaiti parliament passed a law banning women from working between 8:00 P.M. and 7:00 A.M., to protect public morals.

BIRTH

The birth of a child is always a source of great delight and celebration, even more so if the child is a boy. The government gives all parents a cash gift

A family enjoying a day out at an amusement center.

for each baby born, and it continues to pay a monthly allowance until the child marries or gets a job. In modern Kuwait women usually give birth in a hospital rather than at home as in the past. The baby will often be swaddled or wrapped tightly in cloth and will be named when seven days old. Boys are always circumcised, and this is usually done in the hospital at a very young age.

MARRIAGE

Most Kuwaitis marry, as this is considered the most socially acceptable situation for adults. Men typically marry in their mid-20s and women in their early 20s. Mothers assume the responsibility of finding marriage partners for their children. Kuwaitis usually marry partners agreed on by their family, often from the same wider clan group, which means their partner may be a relative. The government pays a grant to every Kuwaiti man intending to marry a Kuwaiti woman; Kuwaiti men marrying foreign women do not receive a grant.

In 2005 Dr. Massouma Mubarak, a female academic and journalist educated in the United States, was appointed as planning minister and minister of state for administrative development affairs.

Muslim men may marry Christian and Jewish women, although it is not encouraged, and they do not need permission from their parents to marry. Muslim women can marry only Muslim men, and they usually need permission from their male guardian to wed. A man may have up to four wives at a time, provided he can treat them all equally. Polygamy, however, is relatively rare. Women can be married to only one man at a time. A man can divorce a woman by stating "I divorce you" three times. He must then pay her a sum agreed upon in the marriage contract so that she can live without him. A woman can divorce her husband only if he does not provide for her.

Once a marriage is likely, the parents will finalize the details. These include an agreed-upon amount of gold jewelry to be given to the woman by the man's family and possibly some money. The cost of the gifts may be as much as $50,000. The official marriage may take place quietly, but it will be considered only an engagement; the couple may be alone with each other but do not yet live together. When they do move in together after at least several months, a big party will mark this stage.

DIVORCE

In the past divorce rates were very low in Kuwait, thanks to the support of the extended family and also because most women were financially dependent. There was also great social shame attached to being divorced, and a woman would generally lose her children to the husband's family. The gradual breakdown of the extended family, greater educational and job opportunities for women, and increasing outside influences, especially during the 1990—91 Gulf War, have contributed to an increase in the divorce rate. In 1972 the divorce rate was 6.5 percent; by 1985 it had increased to 9.4 percent, and by 2005, 36.5 percent. Since then, however, the percentage of divorces has declined: In 2007 the rate of divorce for Kuwaiti couples was 8.8 percent, while the divorce rate for Kuwaiti men married to women

THE WEDDING PARTY

Within a few months, or a year at the most, of the proposal, two wedding parties are held: one for the bride's family and one for the groom's. The groom will wear traditional clothes, and the bride will wear a European wedding dress. Dancing (with partners of the same sex) will celebrate the occasion, which will go on for many hours, with soft drinks, tea, and probably a meal. Kuwaiti families spend as much money as possible on weddings, and this is an important source of social prestige. Hundreds or even thousands of guests may be invited. The government gives all new grooms a loan to finance some of the festivities.

from other nationalities was 4.7 percent and for Kuwaiti women married to foreign men was 15.5 percent.

SAVING FACE

The concept of "face," pertaining to prestige and reputation, exists in Kuwait as it does in the West, but there is an intensity about it in Kuwait that is almost

A Kuwaiti father spending time with his family. Kuwaitis prefer to marry and conduct business within the family.

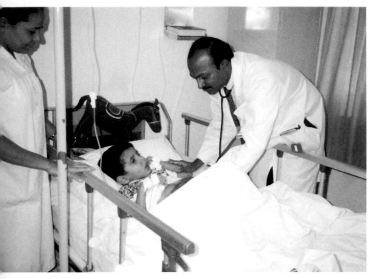

Kuwaitis enjoy excellent health care.

inconceivable to a Westerner. A Kuwaiti spends his life building and maintaining face, and the amount of face that he earns is an indication of the degree to which he serves and protects his family's interests.

Children learn about saving face from early childhood. A child is considered to be an adult when he realizes that his own success, or face, is directly related to that of his family's. Every adult's face is affected by the behavior of his or her relatives. This sense of maintaining face lies behind most behavior in social and business settings. Although becoming rich can add face, visible failure in business loses it, which is why many Kuwaiti men hold on to unsuccessful businesses.

DEATH

Following Muslim tradition, Kuwaitis are buried within 24 hours of death. The body is washed, wrapped in white cloth, and carried by men to the grave, where it is buried without a coffin, facing Mecca. There are usually no flowers, and the grave is marked simply with a small plinth or paving slab. Male mourners do not shave, and women wear black. A memorial service may be held at a mosque. Guests express their condolences over the next 40 days, keeping the bereaved family company.

HEALTH CARE

Kuwait is divided into five health regions, each with a government-run general hospital. There are several specialist hospitals as well. In total 15 hospitals and more than 70 local clinics serve Kuwait's needs, providing 4,700 beds. Primary health care is provided by the state through a network of polyclinics. Medications prescribed by a doctor are free at hospitals and government pharmacies. Dental care is also free.

Kuwait's Ministry of Health employs more than 34,000 people (of whom just over half are Kuwaiti nationals), including 4,400 doctors and more than 10,000 nurses, most of whom are expatriate workers. This means there is one doctor for every 590 people in Kuwait. Any patient with needs that cannot be met in Kuwait will be sent abroad at government expense.

EDUCATION

Nearly 500,000 students, or roughly 20 percent of the entire population, are enrolled in Kuwaiti schools. Until the 1930s education in Kuwait was entirely private, consisting of Koranic schools. Since 1965 there has been free education from kindergarten to graduate school. One-third of state employees are connected to this enormous education system. There are almost 100 private schools, including the English School, which was the first private school to open in Kuwait. Other private schools include Fahaheel al-Watanieh Indian Private School (a collaboration with the Delhi Public School Society of India), the American School of Kuwait, and the American International School. These are only for expatriate workers but come under state supervision. Many teachers are foreigners; in the 1980s more than 70 percent were non-Kuwaiti Arabs. Over the years the government has tried to remedy this situation by training more Kuwaitis and encouraging more women to enter the profession.

Kindergarten is available for all four- and five-year-olds, and education is compulsory (and free) for those ages 6—14. After kindergarten, boys and girls attend separate schools, although the universities are coeducational. Classes are small, rarely with more than 20 students in a class. The school day starts early, at 7:15 A.M., and finishes at 1:00 P.M. All schoolchildren wear uniforms, and there is no school on Thursday and Friday, the Kuwaiti weekend. There is a three-month holiday in summer and short holidays for major

Kuwaiti students in class. The Kuwaiti government has been trying to encourage more Kuwaitis to join the teaching profession.

festivals. Children start studying English in the fifth grade. Extracurricular activities are not as important to Kuwaiti children as to American children, and physical exercise is not part of the curriculum, although the government provides sports clubs and recreation centers.

Kuwait University, which was set up in 1966, has more than 19,000 students, with more than 500 doing postgraduate studies. Kuwait University offers 65 academic programs through its 12 colleges. The faculty consists of nearly 1,300 professors and associate professors, of whom 300 are Kuwaiti citizens. The university offers degrees in arts, sciences, education, commerce, law, engineering, Islamic studies, medicine, and health sciences. All the science and engineering courses are taught in English, but the arts, humanities, and social sciences courses are in Arabic. Most students who wish to pursue postgraduate studies are sent abroad at government expense. The Gulf University for Science and Technology, the first private university established in Kuwait, opened in 2002. The American University of Kuwait opened in 2004, with Dr. Shafeeq al-Ghabra as founding president.

TRADITIONAL KUWAITI HOUSES

Traditional Kuwaiti houses, like many others in the Middle East, present a forbidding front to the world. In the old city, rows of blank, plastered walls give no hint of the houses behind the wooden doors that appear at intervals. These carved and decorated teak doors, with carved posts and lintels, were common around the Gulf, but Kuwaiti doors had distinctive carvings of rosettes.

The plain exterior of the houses has both a practical and a social purpose. Because of the hot climate, it is more practical to live in thick-walled rooms, shaded beneath columned arcades around an open courtyard, than in enclosed spaces. Concealing the courtyard, meanwhile, offers privacy to the women; with no windows they can be totally secluded. Humble exteriors also conceal the possible wealth of the family from jealous eyes.

Traditional houses have an outer area, sometimes with a courtyard and sleeping rooms where male guests can be entertained. For the women there

Kuwait University has a 10-year plan to construct a university city that will provide a modern campus with state-of-the-art facilities for students, academic staff, and other university employees. The new campus will house 40,000 students and cost more than $3 billion to build.

is a smaller and separate inner area, ideally with its own entrance. A staircase leads to the roof, where the family sleeps when the weather is hot. Although air-conditioning means that there is no longer any need for cool courtyards or verandas nor any reason to sleep outside, the separation of public and family quarters remains.

As traditional Kuwaiti houses are made largely of mud, repairs are needed every year after the spring rains. But instead of repairs the houses are often rebuilt. After the oil boom many Kuwaitis did not carry out repairs, and houses were demolished or neglected. Modern houses are now preferred.

THE VILLA

Although some Kuwaitis and almost all expatriate workers live in apartment blocks, most Kuwaitis live in the suburbs of the cities in large houses known as villas. These villas can be built in almost any style, including that of a Spanish hacienda or an Alpine chalet. Almost all villas are white or gray and share certain features. They all have rooftop water tanks and a series of television antennas or satellite dishes. The flat roofs are often surrounded by a wall for added privacy. They are usually square, two or three stories, designed in stone or concrete, and decorated with marble facing, decorative windows, and elaborate facades.

Most are surrounded by a high wall with security gates, and many appear quite ordinary on the outside, a continuation of traditional architecture. The windows are usually shuttered against the heat. Inside the high walls, separate buildings may exist for branches of the family or for the servants. The interiors of houses are spacious, with large reception rooms and high ceilings.

An old gate reflects the traditional architecture of Kuwait City's early buildings.

RELIGION

The Grand Mosque in al-Qibla.

THE VAST MAJORITY OF KUWAITIS are Muslims, as the followers of Islam are called, and their Muslim identity is as important as, if not more so, than their Kuwaiti or Arab identity. To Muslims Islam is much more than a set of beliefs. It offers a complete guide to every aspect of life and influences their daily behavior.

Even though most Kuwaitis are Muslim, other religions are allowed to practice without prejudice.

Five pillars, or requirements, form the basis of Islam: profession of faith, praying five times daily, giving alms, fasting during the month of Ramadan, and making a pilgrimage to Mecca. The five pillars, as well as obligations such as being honest, just, and willing to defend Islam, and prohibitions such as not eating pork, drinking alcohol, or lending money for interest or gambling, form common bonds among Muslims.

Kuwait lies on the Arabian Peninsula, the birthplace of the prophet Muhammed and of Islam, the religion he founded. *Islam* means "to submit" in Arabic. A Muslim submits to the will of God, which was revealed through prophets, including those recognized by Judaism and Christianity. For Muslims the last of these prophets was Muhammed, to whom the Koran, the word

Right: A mosque is not only a place of worship but also a place of religious instruction.

1. shahada (sha-ha-DAH) *Professing faith—that there is no God but Allah, and Muhammed is his prophet—in the form of a recitation in Arabic*

2. salat (sal-AT) *Praying five times a day in the correct manner*

3. zakat (za-KAAT) *Giving alms to the needy or to good causes.*

4. saum (sowm) *Fasting (not even water) between sunrise and sunset for the 28 days of the Islamic month of Ramadan*

5. hajj *Making the pilgrimage to Mecca at least once in a lifetime*

of God, was revealed by the angel Gabriel, in the seventh century of the Christian era.

The prophet Muhammed established Islam when he founded the first Muslim community in Medina, in what is now Saudi Arabia, in A.D. 622. The Islamic calendar starts at this point, so like all other Islamic countries, Kuwait operates with two calendars. Although the Prophet died 10 years later, his followers established a vast empire until the Middle East, North Africa, and parts of Europe were united in the Muslim faith.

PRAYER AND IMPORTANCE OF TIME

The most important daily aspect of Islam to most Muslims is the second pillar, the requirement to pray five times a day. The prayers, which are said in Arabic, are directed toward Mecca. Before praying Muslims must wash their face, arms, head, and feet in a prescribed manner. They must also be ritually clean, in that they should wash thoroughly after certain activities, such as using the toilet. Women are excused from praying when they are menstruating or have recently given birth.

A Koran-reading class. The Koran is considered sacred and is always kept clean, handled gently with clean hands, and kept in a special cloth or box.

Although prayers can be performed up to an hour before or after the set times, it is considered best to pray on time. Prayers can be offered almost anywhere, even in the street, but many men, and some women, prefer to pray in a mosque. Prayer times are announced from loudspeakers on the minarets of the many mosques, and most people will stop work to pray. All public places, such as airports or shopping malls, provide a place to pray. In case the direction of Mecca is not indicated, many Kuwaitis carry a small compass. Adult men try to attend the midday prayers at a mosque on Fridays, the Muslim holy day. This is not just a time for prayer but also a social occasion and a chance to attend a lecture by a religious figure.

THE GLORIOUS KORAN

The prophet Muhammed was not the author of the Koran but its messenger. Muslims consider the Koran the final word of God, replacing and correcting the Old and New Testaments and any other holy books. During the Prophet's lifetime, the Koran was memorized in parts, but after his death it was written down, and it remains unchanged. It is arranged in 114 *suwar*, or named chapters, divided into 6,236 *ayat*, or verses. It has no clear beginning or end; all the parts are interconnected by rhyme, rhythm, and meaning. Not even a single dot or letter can be changed without altering the entire text. All Muslims study the Koran, and children in Kuwaiti schools memorize all or parts of it and study its meaning and interpretation.

THE PILGRIMAGE: THE AIM OF A LIFETIME

All Muslims aim to make the pilgrimage, or hajj, to Mecca at least once in a lifetime. Kuwaitis are fortunate in that they live so close to Mecca, which is in Saudi Arabia, on the other side of the Arabian Peninsula. Muslims who make the pilgrimage have the honor of adding the title hajji, for a man, or *hajjieh*, for a woman, before their names.

The pilgrimage is undertaken at a certain time of the year, and visits outside this period do not count as the real pilgrimage. All business must be set in order before departure, a leftover from when the journey would take

Many of the stories from the Old and New Testaments appear in the Koran, often in a slightly different form. For example, in the story of Abraham's testing by God, it is his son Ismael, and not Isaac, whom Abraham is ready to sacrifice at God's demand. The only woman's name in the Koran is that of Mary (Maryam in Arabic), the mother of Jesus (Esau), who is revered as a prophet. These and many other names in the Koran are quite familiar to Christians in their anglicized forms.

Thousands of Muslims congregate in Mecca every year for the pilgrimage.

A PROPHET AND A MODEL FOR MUSLIMS

The life of the prophet Muhammed is considered to be a model for all Muslims. Much of what he said and did was recorded by writers, and these traditions, together with the Koran, are used by Muslims as a guide to living.

Born in A.D. 570, he was a poor orphan who later worked as a trader. When he was 25 he married his employer, a rich widow of 40 named Khadijah, who became the first Muslim. After she died, leaving him with a daughter, Fatima, he did not remarry for many years, until his role as a leader of the Muslims led him to do so a few times for a variety of reasons. He left no adult sons. Many Muslims claim to be descendants of his family. They call themselves sayyids *and are honored by other Muslims.*

Although he became wealthy, the prophet Muhammed led a simple life and was famed for his kindness to his family and friends as well as to anyone who approached him for help. Although Muslims are proud of the way he led his life and of his achievements, they are careful to distinguish this from any notion that they follow him instead of God and Islam.

months, if not years. Throughout the journey pilgrims must not use soap or perfume, cut their hair or nails, or damage anything in nature, and men and women must not sleep together. All men wear two white, seamless sheets of cloth, and women keep their faces unveiled.

The rituals of the pilgrimage, which commemorate certain incidents in the life of the Prophet, last nine days, and each year roughly 2 million people perform these ritualistic actions. The pilgrimage climaxes with the slaughter of an animal, which is then given to the poor, and the male pilgrims shave their heads. Many Muslims then visit the town of Medina, where the prophet Muhammed is buried.

THE SHIITES

The majority of Kuwaitis are Sunni Muslims, but a significant minority—up to 30 percent of Kuwaitis—are Shiites. The division between Sunnis and Shiites appeared soon after the death of the prophet Muhammed over the question of who should be the leader. The Shiites felt that Ali, the Prophet's son-in-law, and his descendants should be chosen as leaders.

Muslim prayer times: *salat ul-fajr* (dawn or sunrise), *salat ul-zuhr* (midday), *salat ul-asr* (midafternoon), *salat al-maghrib* (sunset), and *salat al-isha* (90 minutes after sunset).

Calls to prayer can be heard from the minarets of mosques.

Today Shiites are a majority only in Iran. Sunni and Shiite Muslims both follow the basic five pillars of Islam but differ on the interpretation of Islamic teachings, tend not to intermarry, and pray in different mosques. The Shiites have an additional calendar of religious festivals; these are related to events in the lives of Ali and other imams (religious leaders).

THE MOSQUE

There are mosques in most public buildings in Kuwait and in places such as airports, offices, and shopping malls. The most obvious external feature is the minaret, from where the calls for prayer are announced. An indispensable feature is a place where worshipers can wash before praying. A mosque has no furniture, but it is well carpeted so that the worshipers can kneel, sit, and stand in comfort while praying. There is usually a pulpit so that a prayer leader can give a sermon after leading the prayers.

The mosque is clearly oriented in the direction of Mecca. The symbol of Islam, a crescent and star, usually decorates the dome. Mosques are also often used as places for teaching, meeting, and quiet meditation.

In Kuwait women have special rooms or galleries in many mosques so as to ensure that they will not be seen by men. Non-Muslims can visit mosques, as long as they are People of the Book—in other words, Jews and Christians. While in a mosque they must observe the same rules as Muslims. They must remove their shoes to ensure that the floor remains clean and wear clothes that cover their arms and legs. Women must cover their hair, and men are encouraged to wear a hat or other head covering.

THE GRAND MOSQUE

There are more than 70 mosques in Kuwait, from simple neighborhood ones with space for up to 1,000 worshipers to grand buildings that can accommodate many thousands of people. Many mosques were damaged during the Iraqi occupation, but one mosque that has been fully restored and that Kuwaitis are very proud of is al-Masjid al-Kabir, the Grand Mosque.

Construction of this 215,278-square-foot (20,000-square-m) building began in 1979 and was completed in 1986 at a cost of about $43 million. It lays claim to being the world's most innovative mosque. It can accommodate 10,500 male and 950 female worshipers and has places for 106 people to perform their ritual ablutions at a time, as well as parking spaces for 500 cars. The mosque provides not only a place of worship but also a massive library and reading hall, as well as a conference center and a reception hall for VIPs.

Its architecture uses various traditional Islamic styles, and the building was constructed using modern technology, combining reinforced concrete, natural stone, and decorative marble. The mosque's main hall boasts 144 windows that provide full daytime illumination. The center dome in the main hall, which is 141 feet (43 m) high, is engraved with the 99 names of Allah in intricate Arabic calligraphy. Engraving panels in wooden doors with quotations from the Koran in Arabic calligraphy and Islamic design is a Gulf tradition and can be seen in the mosque's 21 teak doors, which were carved by Indian artisans.

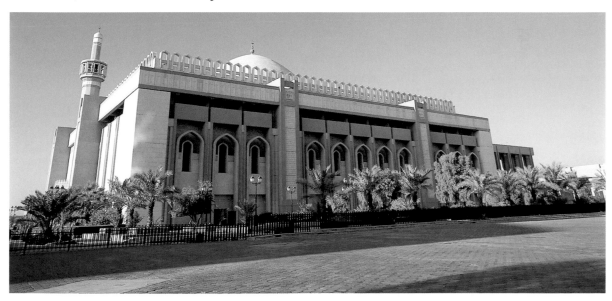

LANGUAGE

A Kuwaiti man reading a local newspaper.

ARABIC IS THE NATIVE LANGUAGE

of about 70 percent of Kuwait's population and the sacred language of all Muslims, who make up 85 percent of Kuwait's population. It is the official language of Kuwait, and all government documents and notices are in modern standard Arabic.

English, particularly American English, is the second language for most educated Kuwaitis. It is important in business circles, but getting around with just English could be difficult, although street signs and many shop signs are in both English and Arabic.

Many other languages are spoken in Kuwait, reflecting the diverse origins of the many expatriates in the country. In particular Farsi

Billboards of political candidates line the sidewalks of a street in Kuwait.

(Persian), standard Hindi, and Punjabi are widely heard in the streets and souks, or markets.

Arabic is spoken by more than 200 million people in the world and is the official language of 26 countries, as well as one of the six official languages of the United Nations. It is an important link between Kuwaitis and the rest of the Middle East and North Africa. Three main forms of Arabic exist: classical, the language of the Koran; modern standard, which is used for writing in all countries and for communication between Arabs from different regions; and colloquial or spoken Arabic.

Each Arabic region has its own dialect; that of Kuwait is a mixture of bedouin dialects and the dialect of the Gulf traders. It is liberally mixed with Persian, Indian, Egyptian, and American words, making it sound different from other Arabic dialects. Its sounds are a little softer and less glottal (the sound that is made in the back of the throat). This dialect is considered by Gulf Arabs to be somewhat new and hip, in keeping with the image of Kuwait as being a very modern country.

ARABIC: THE LANGUAGE OF GOD

Arabic is more than a mother tongue to Kuwaitis. For all Muslims it is the sacred language in which the Koran was revealed by God to the prophet Muhammed. *Koran* means "recitation" in Arabic. Many Muslims believe the Koran should not be translated into other languages but read only in Arabic, as it is perfect in its original form. A Muslim prays in Arabic, whatever his or her mother tongue, and all Muslims aim to be able to read and recite the Koran in Arabic. Arabic is possibly the main cultural link among the world's 1 billion Muslims, of whom only one-sixth are Arabs. Many common Arabic expressions are derived from the Muslim faith and are used throughout the Muslim world. Examples of common expressions include the following:

as-salaamu alaykum	peace be upon you (used as a greeting)
wa-alaykum salaam	and peace be upon you too (the standard reply)
alhamdillallah	thanks be to God (used whenever good news is given)

bismillah	in the name of God (used before eating or undertaking many activities)
insha'allah	God willing (used after every statement concerning the future)
mashallah	blessings of God (used whenever something is positive)
ya allah	with God's help
wa allah	by God; truthfully

Many Kuwaitis like to decorate their homes, offices, and cars with these expressions or with verses taken from the Koran. These are written in beautifully flowing calligraphy.

LEARNING ARABIC

Arabic has 10 sounds that do not exist in English, although some of these sounds are used in other languages such as Spanish. Arabic grammar is

A teacher conducting an evening Koranic class. Arabic is a phonetic language.

Possibly the most commonly used polite expression in Kuwait is *ahlan wa sahlan*, or "at home and at ease," used roughly to mean "welcome." This was originally used by the bedouin to greet travelers but is now used by hosts, businesspeople, and tradespeople to mean "relax, be comfortable."

ARABIC FOR ENGLISH SPEAKERS

Arabic is not entirely strange to English speakers, nor to the speakers of many other languages, as many Arabic words are used in other languages. This is partly because of the discoveries made by Islamic scientists and philosophers, who wrote in Arabic; for example, "alcohol" is from al-kol, used by the Arab chemists in the Middle Ages. "Algebra" is from al-jabr, as Islamic mathematicians invented many mathematical ideas. El, a word for "the" in Spanish, comes from when part of Spain was occupied by the Arabs; al is Arabic for "the."

The numbers used in English are called Arabic numerals, as they use combinations of nine figures and zero, or decimal figures, an idea that came from the Arabs via India. There are similarities with the Arabic versions, especially in the numbers 0, 1, and 9.

When Arabic words are translated into English, it is often necessary to use more than one letter to indicate the Arabic sound, and it takes practice to learn to pronounce these sounds.

complex, but it has some similarities with Greek and Latin. All nouns are either male or female, and the form of the noun differs according to whether you are referring to one, two, or more of that item. Thus it can be hard to identify a noun unless you know all three versions, which can be very different from one another.

Arabic script is written from right to left, and the language is entirely phonetic—that is, it is written exactly as it sounds. The writing is always joined fluidly, and there are no capital letters. Each letter has up to three forms, depending on whether it appears at the beginning, in the middle, or at the end of a word. There are, however, fewer letters than in the English alphabet. Not all vowels are written, as there are fewer vowel sounds than in English, but little marks can indicate the vowel sounds for beginners or in foreign words.

YOU ARE WHAT YOU ARE CALLED

Kuwaitis' names are clues to their ancestry. Kuwaitis have a profound sense of their heritage, and many can trace their ancestors to the clans who arrived with the Bani Utub. A few can trace their origins to clans that already lived in the area. Some prominent families arrived later from other Gulf states, and those of Persian origin arrived mostly during the late 19th and early 20th centuries. Kuwaiti names tell us a great deal about the person. They indicate his or her parentage, clan, or ethnic origin, and so his or her social importance.

The names of a Kuwaiti man or woman will always follow a set order: a given name, the father's name, and then the surname—for example, Mohammed Abdullah al-Shayah is Mohammed, son of Abdullah, of the Shayah family. The name of a grandfather may be inserted after the father's name—for example, Mohammed Abdullah al-Jabir al-Shayah's grandfather's name is Jabir. Generally speaking, the more important the person, the longer the name. The surname is always that of a common ancestor, and all persons with that name will be related, however distantly.

An exception is Kuwaitis of Iranian origin, whose surname may indicate their approximate place of origin. For example, the surname Behbani means the person's ancestors belonged to the village of Behban.

A Kuwaiti child must be named so that his parentage and clan are apparent.

ARABIC NAMES

Almost all Kuwaitis have Arabic first names, often the name of their parents or grandparents, and most names have religious connotations. These include the names of the prophets or saints, such as Mohammed, Yusef (Joseph), and Musa (Moses), and names of devotion to God, such as Abdullah ("slave of God") and Abdul Rahman ("slave of the merciful one"). Other names indicate good qualities, such as Mubarak ("good fortune"), and Salem ("good health"). Great thought is given to choosing names, often with the help of the Koran, and they can reflect events at the time of birth or the parents' hopes for their child. Many men's names have a feminine version, usually by adding the female endings eh/yeh—for example, Amir is a male name, while Amireh is the female version. So women may have names with similar meanings to men's names. They can also be named after female religious figures, such as Maryam (Mary) and Aisha and Khadijah (the wives of the prophet Muhammed). Additionally, many women's names have lovely meanings, such as Jamileh ("beautiful"; the male version is Jamil), Sultana ("queen"), and Yasmina ("jasmine").

Women also use their family and father's names. They do not change their names when they marry, as they will always belong to the same tribe and father all their lives. Because marriages between cousins are common, many couples do share the same surname, but the father's name will, of course, be different.

NAMES WITHIN THE FAMILY In most respects Kuwaiti names follow the general Arab conventions. It is an essential part of Arabic and Islamic culture to honor one's parents, and no one can change or give up his or her father's name. For this reason adoption is frowned upon, as a child must always use his or her father's name. People may be referred to as son (*ibn*) or daughter (*bint*) of someone when they are introduced for the first time—for example, Mohammed ibn Abdullah.

Another custom within the family and among friends is to refer to people as mother (*umm*) or father (*abu*) of their eldest son. Thus Abdullah and his wife, Khadijah, once their son Mohammed is born, may be thereafter referred to as Abu Mohammed and Umm Mohammed. This indicates the pride that Arabs have in their children, especially the firstborn son. Many husbands and wives refer to each other in this way. Although it is possible to be referred to as the parent of a girl child, this is very unusual and done only if there are no sons in the marriage. The family, and one's place within it, is really the key to people's names in Kuwait.

POLITE RITUALS

Arabic has many expressions that are part of polite formalities. An acquaintance is greeted enthusiastically, and lengthy inquiries will be made after his or her health and that of the family or any mutual friends. This may last for several minutes. A man will not usually refer to another man's wife unless they are related, but he may ask after the family in general. It is very rude to rush straight to business without the proper formalities. Generally before business of any sort, tea or coffee will be offered. Kuwaitis are very polite and sociable, and this extends to all areas of life, not just social activities.

Men are demonstrative to each other in public, but face and honor must be maintained at all times.

Kuwaitis are so polite that they rarely use the word "no," so as not to cause disappointment. Things are usually *insha'allah*, or "God willing." This is part of the general Kuwaiti culture of avoiding unpleasantness. Kuwaitis tend to conceal their anger in public; it would be a serious loss of face for a person to show any lack of personal control. Kuwaitis show their displeasure in subtle ways, by slight gestures or a faint lack of enthusiasm. These are all easily detected by other Kuwaitis.

Kuwaitis are generally very concerned about their honor and social appearance, or face. This means that they behave in a generally dignified manner at all times. Adult men walk with dignity, sit up straight when in company, and pay great attention to their appearance. Kuwaiti men and women do not touch each other in public. It is common, however, to see women showing great affection to each other in public, while men kiss and hug each other in greeting. Men do not kiss women to whom they are not related. Women do not generally shake hands with men.

THE MEDIA

Kuwait has among the most open media in the Arab world, and Kuwaiti newspapers often criticize government policy. In 2007 Kuwait was ranked second in the Middle East, after Israel, in the Freedom of Press Index.

Kuwaiti journalists enjoy much greater freedom to report than most other Arab journalists. Much of the media is state owned, although some private newspapers are run under the supervision of the Ministry of Communications. The state-owned Kuwait News Agency is the largest media house in the country. The Ministry of Information does censor books, films, magazines, and any other imported material that is considered to offend Islamic or Arab sensibilities.

There are five daily newspapers in Arabic and two in English—*The Arab Times* and *The Kuwait Times*. There are also newspapers in standard Hindi and Urdu. More than 70 magazines are published in Kuwait. Newspapers are not cheap, but a slightly greater percentage of people in Kuwait read newspapers than in the United States. This reflects the interest that Kuwaitis have in the rest of the world.

Kuwait has 10 satellite television channels, of which four are controlled by the Ministry of Information. State-owned Kuwait Television first offered color broadcasts in 1974 and today operates three television channels. Popular private channels include al-Rai and al-Watan. Most people have satellite dishes and so receive television programs from all over the world. Television channels that show Egyptian films and programs are very popular.

There are no private radio stations in Kuwait, but the state channels broadcast all types of music—Arabic and foreign, old and modern. Government-funded Radio Kuwait also broadcasts daily informative programs in four foreign languages—Farsi, Urdu, Tagalog, and English. In 2002, Kuwaiti radio stations began broadcasting 24 hours a day. Every evening a channel broadcasts news and other programs in English, and American Armed Forces Radio broadcasts from Doha, the capital of Qatar, to the north of Kuwait City.

There are more than 700,000 Internet users in Kuwait, so many people are able to get international news, entertainment, and information online.

A board provides information in Arabic on seatbelt safety.

A press law forbids insulting references to God and the prophet Muhammed.

ARTS

A Kuwaiti craftsman carves out
a wooden souvenir dhow.

KUWAIT HAS A NATIONAL Council for Culture, Arts, and Letters (NCCAL), founded in 1974, which is responsible for culture, fine arts, the national heritage, and public libraries. The government is dedicated to developing all aspects of Kuwaiti arts, and a great deal is invested in rediscovering lost art forms and encouraging new ones.

Many traditional arts were derived from craft activities, but a number of these are no longer practiced. The NCCAL organizes an annual cultural

Girls learning to weave. The Kuwaiti government is trying to revive dying art forms.

Kuwait's art scene is one that is rich and thriving. The government has even set up an agency to aid in the development of contemporary art as well as the preservation of traditional Kuwaiti art forms such as weaving. Islam has also had a deep impact on Kuwaiti art, and this is reflected in forms such as painting, carving, and calligraphy.

festival known as the Qurain Festival, through which orchestras and artists from Kuwait and the rest of the Arab world put their work on public display.

As Kuwait is a deeply Islamic country, both its traditional and modern art forms are profoundly influenced by its religious heritage. In the past, to paint or show human figures was not allowed, as these might be used for pagan worship. This meant that abstract ways to praise God reflected the highest forms of Islamic art. In the performing arts, it is considered inappropriate for men to listen to women sing or watch them dance. The majority of musicians are men, and dancing, apart from performances by folkloric troupes, tends to be a single gender activity. The Folklore Preservation Center collects and records Kuwaiti folklore. Since 1982, folklore has been included as a subject for students of music, theater, and fine arts in Kuwaiti schools.

BEDOUIN ARTS

Bedouin art is the most prominent expression of Kuwaiti folk art. The best examples are the textiles woven from sheep's wool; these are called *sadu* (sa-DOO). Wool is hand-dyed and spun and then woven into geometric designs

Bedouin performing the Ardha, a traditional war dance.

BEDOUIN INDUSTRY

The traditional bedouin name for a tent translates to "house of hair," as both the tent and all its contents were woven by women out of camel hair or wool from sheep. The women wove flat rugs and cushion covers, which were stuffed with clothes and other household cloths, to furnish the tent. Large woven cloths were used to cover piles of bedding, which could be used to lean on during the day as well as to divide the tent into rooms. The women also wove saddlebags to hold their possessions between camps, as well as decorative bridles and saddles for the camels. All this was achieved with portable wooden looms and local materials. Tools were made out of gazelle horns; few bedouin women owned a pair of scissors.

The wool used for weaving was spun and dyed by hand. The women managed to fit these activities in between cooking and chores such as milking, making clothes, and caring for their children. The finished products traditionally belonged to the men, who could sell them or keep them for their own use.

on a portable loom. Traditionally bedouin women wove black tents of camel hair with decorative *sadu* side flaps, cushions, and saddlebags for camels. As most bedouin now live in housing settlements, there are few women learning this craft. In 1980 al-Sadu House was established to keep this dying art alive, and bedouin women are employed to demonstrate the craft.

Another bedouin art form is the Ardha, a dance in which the agile manipulation of a sword accompanies drums, tambourines, and poetic songs. Folkloric dance troupes are supported by the government and appear regularly on television and at social occasions such as weddings. The Kuwaiti Television Folklore Troupe has presented Kuwaiti bedouin dance and folklore at many world festivals.

JEWELRY

Gold jewelry has long been a vital part of Kuwaiti culture. For the bedouin, gold and silver are a portable bank balance, and women are given large quantities of jewelry when they marry, just in case they need to support themselves.

Kuwaiti women shopping for gold jewelry.

Jewelry is the most common gift on such special occasions as a wedding, the birth of a child, and a birthday. The designs of gold jewelry are elaborate and include both traditional and modern touches. The latest creations of famous jewelers in Paris are copied immediately in Kuwait, and it would be hard to tell that these are not the originals.

Many Indian craftsmen also work in Kuwait, and a large section of the souk is filled with passageways lined with dazzling gold displays in shop windows. Since the early days of pearling in Kuwait, its jewelers have been skilled at creating jewelry using pearls, as well as imported gemstones.

SCULPTURE

The art of sculpture was introduced in Kuwait in 1963, when a course was offered at the state art school, the Free Atelier. Today there is much interest in creating sculpture in Kuwait, especially since Kuwait's most famous sculptor, Sami Mohammed, won a design contest to beautify Safat Square in Kuwait City. The winning statue is a big, open shell, 29.5 feet (9 m) high with a diameter of 5 feet (1.5 m), enclosing a stainless steel pearl. The sculpture represents Kuwait's traditional links with the sea.

CALLIGRAPHY

Calligraphy, the art of beautiful writing, is one of the most-developed art forms throughout the Muslim world. Islam discourages art forms showing humans or even animals. Calligraphy avoids this restriction and serves to glorify God, as verses from the Koran are the words usually chosen. The most commonly chosen verse is the Bismillah, which is the opening verse of every chapter of the Koran, calling upon God, the most merciful and compassionate.

AN ARTISTS' REFUGE

The Bayt Lothan Arts and Craft Center opened in 1994. Formerly an old Kuwaiti house that belonged to the late emir Sheikh Sabah al-Salim al-Sabah, it was restored by his daughter, Sheikha Amal Sabah III al-Salim al-Sabah. The center provides artists and the public with a place to pursue and explore their interests in art.

The center also aims to preserve Kuwait's heritage. Anyone over the age of four can attend courses in fine arts, music, handicrafts, Islamic calligraphy, drama, and photography. All the instructors are Kuwaitis. Music is the most popular area of study, especially piano, flute, violin, and oud, a type of Arab guitar.

Regular exhibitions offer artwork for sale at reasonable prices as well as inform the public about new areas of art and the humanities. Other activities include public-safety education and the sponsorship of new poets and musicians.

Calligraphy is used as a decoration for books, manuscripts, buildings, and household items. It is rendered on paper, leather, stone, glass, china, pottery, ivory, and textiles. Calligraphic designs can be woven into carpets and fabric. They can be rendered in various forms and shapes, from animals to stars to flowers. There are several accepted styles of calligraphy, and artists are always working to perfect them as well as to develop new ones.

THE THEATER

Like folk arts, the theater has received attention from the Kuwaiti government. The Higher Institute for Theatrical Arts trains actors and performers to degree level and encourages awareness and appreciation of theater in Kuwait. The country has four theater companies sponsored by the government.

ARCHITECTURE

Most Kuwaitis probably feel that their greatest contribution to the arts is in the world of modern architecture. In the past, all architectural undertakings

Although Kuwait has several movie theaters, satellite television is more popular for family entertainment, and giant satellite dishes crowd roofs and balconies of many houses.

THE KUWAIT NATIONAL MUSEUM

The Kuwait National Museum is the most important repository of the artifacts of Kuwaiti historical and cultural life. It includes art galleries and displays of antiquities and handicrafts. All the antiquities from archaeological expeditions are displayed.

Part of the museum complex, the Museum of Islamic Arts, once housed a priceless collection of more than 20,000 items of Islamic art—huge doors, carpets, rare books, manuscripts, china, jewels—covering 12 centuries. Founded in 1983, this collection, called Dar al-Athar al-Islamiyyah (House of Islamic Antiquities), still constitutes one of the most comprehensive collections of Islamic art in the world. The collection was started by patron of the arts Sheikh Nasser al-Sabah and his wife, Sheikha Hussa al-Sabah. In 1991 all the artifacts were taken or destroyed by the Iraqi invaders, who also demolished the buildings. The museum has since been restored, however, and most of the artifacts have been returned from Iraq (although some pieces had been damaged by rough handling). In 1997 Muhallab II, a replica of the beautiful 1930s trading dhow that sat in the front yard of the museum before it was burned by Iraqi forces, was constructed on-site and is now open to visitors.

in Kuwait were foreign ventures, but now the country has enough trained architects, many with experience overseas, to design its own buildings. Although architectural remnants of old Kuwait remain, and the government is keen on restoring them, Kuwait lacks the older, elaborate architecture found in many other Arab countries. Local architecture consisted of simple mud and stone single-story houses. They were designed for function rather than form and equipped to withstand the extreme summer heat. Modern architecture in Kuwait, however, has adventurously combined the need for protection from the elements with Islamic Arab architectural and decorative styles and modern materials and construction techniques.

The skyline of Kuwait City is dominated by the country's most famous landmark, Kuwait Towers, strategically located at the point where Kuwait juts farthest into the Gulf. The towers of this 161-foot (49-m) building have a useful function. Two of the three blue towers are water reservoirs. The largest of the towers rises to a height of 614 feet (187 m) and is home to a revolving restaurant and observation platform.

A KUWAITI ARTIST

Born in 1952 in Kuwait City, Thuraya al-Baqsami began her artistic career at an early age. In 1969 she became a member of the Kuwaiti Art Society and was awarded a bronze medal in 1971 by the Kuwaiti Society of Formative Artists. She received her academic training in Cairo at the College of Fine Arts during the 1970s before moving to study in Moscow in 1981.

She received the Golden Palm Leaf award from the GCC Biennale in Riyadh in 1989 and in Doha in 1992. Her work is held in public and private collections throughout Asia, the Middle East, the United States, and Europe. She also received an award in literature from the Kuwait Foundation for the Advancement of Sciences in 1993 for her collection of short stories, Cellar Candles, *and the State Award for Children's Literature in 1997 for a book of children's stories,* The Recollection of Small Kuwaiti Fatuma.

A peace campaigner, Thuraya al-Baqsami considers art to be one of the most powerful means of promoting peace. She has also worked hard to promote women's rights in the Arab world through her work.

In the city center, Liberation Tower is currently the tallest building in Kuwait, standing 1,220 feet (372 m) high at its pinnacle. Completed in 1993, it was renamed from the Kuwait Telecommunication Tower to mark the liberation from the Iraqi occupation in 1991. It is seen by Kuwaitis as a symbol of the country's renaissance since the liberation.

From the 1950s, under a series of master plans, most of old Kuwait was demolished, leaving only the gates to the old city walls. A modern city was built, divided into zones for different commercial activities and for different groups of people to settle in, surrounded by a ring of green parks. Kuwait City, as well as the other cities, became a showpiece for outstanding modern architecture, built in tandem with roads and other public utilities. Many tall water towers, which are often distinctively designed and decorated, punctuate the skyline, as do futuristic, commercial tower blocks. The best example of the blending of the modern with the classically Arabian is the National Assembly Building, which is almost an exact replica of a bedouin tent.

LEISURE

Two Kuwaiti girls enjoying a ride on the ferris wheel at a local fair.

KUWAITIS HAVE ALWAYS SPENT most of their leisure time socializing with their families and their close friends, who are also usually relatives. They do this mostly at home, and particularly in the *diwaniyahs*, or regular social meetings, which are an essential part of Kuwaiti social, political, and cultural life. Sharing food and refreshments is an integral part of most socializing in Kuwait.

Kuwaitis spend most of their leisure time with relatives and friends of the same sex, although within the close family circle and among certain social groups, men and women may socialize together. Kuwaitis love to talk, on the telephone or face to face, and relationships depend on regular and frequent exchanges.

As Kuwaitis have a lot of wealth and leisure time, a thriving leisure and entertainment industry has emerged in the past few years. As it does with most other aspects of Kuwaiti life, the government sees to the provision

Kuwaitis have a lot of leisure time, and most of it is spent with their family and friends. Other pastimes that they enjoy include sports, shopping, and going to entertainment centers.

Right: Youths enjoying a game of soccer. Soccer is a popular sport in Kuwait.

of leisure activities for the people. There are no nightclubs in Kuwait, and the unsupervised mixing of the sexes is frowned upon by conservative Kuwaitis. If young people wish to go out and meet other young people, they do so in American-style coffee shops such as Starbucks or in one of the international hotels.

SPORTS

The government has invested heavily in promoting sports as a healthy pursuit for young people. There are six world-class stadiums in Kuwait. Kuwait's greatest international success has been in soccer, when the national team reached the final qualifying round of the World Cup in 1982, in France. It had previously won the Asian Cup in 1980. Swimming and equestrian competitors have also achieved international success.

There are more cricket teams in Kuwait than all other sporting groups combined. Other popular sports include squash, rugby, baseball, and fishing.

All major companies, ministries, and enterprises have their own sports clubs, which often own private beaches. Competitions may be arranged between clubs.

Soft leather hoods cover the heads of falcons to prevent them from being distracted.

Figure skating and ice hockey are popular, especially in summer. There are several air-conditioned indoor ice rinks; the largest can seat 1,600 spectators. Windsurfing, scuba diving, waterskiing, and Jet Ski racing are also popular. Speedboat racing is a modern version of the dhow races that made Kuwait famous in the region.

FALCONRY Some traditional sports grew out of the activities of the desert. For example, falconry arose from the necessity to supplement a meager diet of dates, milk, and bread and eventually evolved into a major sport. Hunting parties used to pursue their quarry on horseback, but four-wheel-drive vehicles are now used. Wild female falcons are trapped and trained for the hunting season, which begins in late fall. A trained falcon can catch up to five birds, such as bustards and curlews, in a hunting session. This sport ends at sunset, when the booty is cleaned, roasted over a fire, and eaten in the desert.

Gambling is not allowed at horse races, but generous prizes are awarded to the winners and participants.

CAMEL RACING Camels were important to bedouin Arabs, as they were the main source of transportation, textiles, meat, and milk. Traditionally the bedouin would demonstrate the superiority of their camels' bloodlines in a race. Slender, long-legged breeds were bred specially for racing, and there are official racetracks, as well as desert tracks. A camel's training begins at six months, and while a male camel's career will last up to 10 years, a female's will go on for more than 20. Racing camels are fed special foods, such as oats, dates, and cow's milk.

HORSE RACING The Arabian horse is a famed racing breed and one of the most ancient of tamed horses. It has a distinctive appearance, with a short back, a small head with a concave profile, large intelligent eyes, and a tail that it carries high. Although the Arabian horse is bred for racing, it is also used to lighten and improve the heavier breeds. All thoroughbred horses are descendants of Arabian stallions. The bedouin have bred Arabian horses for centuries. They are always prized, and good specimens are traditional gifts between Arab leaders. Both Arabian and thoroughbred racehorses compete in Kuwait.

SHOPPING: A UNIVERSAL PASTIME

Shopping is a national pastime, and almost any item can be purchased in Kuwait, except banned items such as alcohol. Men are as keen as women on shopping, and shopping malls such as the Avenues, Souk Sharq, Salhiyah, and al-Mutthana malls in Kuwait City and the Zahra mall in al-Salmiya provide an American-style shopping experience. These complexes sell consumer goods; food is found primarily in neighborhood supermarkets. Kuwaitis tend to go to malls for entertainment, as these have restaurants, cafés, and fountains.

Kuwaitis in a shopping center.

Shopping is often a family activity. Entire families will visit malls, perhaps combining a shopping trip with a meal at a restaurant.

The Old Souk in Kuwait City, which is actually not more than 70 years old, offers something closer to the traditional style of shopping. It consists of covered passages and open stalls, divided into sections according to the products sold, such as fish, vegetables, clothing, and household goods. Many stalls sell only one type of item, such as knives or olives. Tailors have shops in the souk where they make clothes.

Many entertainment facilities are family-oriented and cater especially to children.

HOTELS, PARKS, AND ENTERTAINMENT CENTERS

Much social life takes place in the country's leading hotels, such as the Hyatt, the Meridien, and the Hilton, all of which have sports facilities and restaurants. Many people meet in the coffee bars or visit the exhibitions. Hotels are the most common location for lavish weddings.

Kuwaiti families like to walk or sit in parks, especially after dark, when it is cooler. Starting from the Kuwait Towers and stretching nearly 15 miles (24 km) along the shore of the Gulf is the Waterfront Project. This park combines attractive brick-and-concrete walkways with rest facilities, playgrounds, and food concessions. The waterfront is lit at night, and there are many entertainment facilities for children, including a miniature train ride.

Entertainment City, which is in the middle of the desert near Doha Village, 12 miles (19 km) west of Kuwait City, is a Disneyland-style theme park offering 40 rides, games, and shows with three themes: Arab World, International World, and Future World. Although this multimillion-dollar complex was destroyed by the Iraqis, it has since been reconstructed.

The oldest resort in Kuwait is on Faylaka Island, just minutes by hovercraft from Kuwait City.

FESTIVALS

Two Kuwaiti girls dressed up for a marriage festival.

THE FESTIVALS OF KUWAIT ARE basically those of Sunni Islam. The Islamic calendar is based on the lunar month, which is only 29 or 30 days long, so there are only 354 days, not 365 days, in a cycle of 12 Islamic months.

Thus festivals do not fall on the same date of the Western calendar each year; they move forward by around 11 days every year. It takes 32.5 years before a festival once again falls on the same date in the Western calendar. For this reason festivals are not associated with any particular time of year, as are Christian festivals, but can fall in any season.

Kuwait observes the Western New Year's holiday as a courtesy to its many foreign residents, and a National Day (February 25). Since the Iraqi invasion and Kuwait's subsequent liberation in February 1991, Liberation Day is celebrated on February 26.

Non-Muslim expatriates living in Kuwait are free to celebrate their own festivals, as are the Shiites, but employers are not required to grant them those days as holidays.

Right: Kuwaiti children dressed in national colors in celebration of National Day.

THE ISLAMIC CALENDAR

The Islamic year begins with the anniversary of the prophet Muhammed's flight from Mecca to Medina in A.D. 622. The 12 months of the Islamic calendar are as follows:

1. Muharram	4. Rabi al-thani	7. Rajab	10. Shawwal
2. Safar	5. Jumada al-awwal	8. Sha'ban	11. Dhu'l-Qa'dah
3. Rabi al-awwal	6. Jumada al-thani	9. Ramadan	12. Dhu'l-Hijja

THE ISLAMIC FESTIVAL CALENDAR

There are two major Islamic holidays in Kuwait: Eid al-Fitr, which occurs at the end of Ramadan, a month of fasting, and Eid al-Adha, or the Festival of the Sacrifice, about three months later. The start of the Islamic year is a minor holiday with little religious significance and merits only a day's holiday, whereas *Eid* indicates a three- or four-day holiday. Other one-day holidays include the prophet Muhammed's birthday, which falls in the third month

Liberation Day is one of Kuwait's few patriotic holidays, and it allows Kuwaitis to remember the great sacrifices that were made in gaining liberation from the Iraqi occupation.

Kuwaiti children buying fireworks in Kuwait City in anticipation of Eid al-Fitr.

of the Islamic year, and the Ascension of the Prophet in the seventh month, when Muhammed was taken to heaven by God to view the world.

RAMADAN, A WELCOME TEST OF ENDURANCE

The month of Ramadan commemorates the first revelation of the Koran to the prophet Muhammed. It is a time for prayer and fasting. In 1991 Ramadan began as Kuwait was liberated from Iraqi forces, and since then it has an even deeper meaning for most Kuwaitis.

Although it is known roughly each year when Ramadan will begin, its exact start occurs as the new moon is sighted and ends with the appearance of the next new moon. This slight uncertainty adds to the excitement for Muslims, who look forward to this special time, despite its hard tests. During the 29 or 30 days of Ramadan, all Muslims must pray on two extra occasions every day, read the Koran, be particularly kind and helpful, and try to fast from dawn to sunset. This means not eating or drinking, not even water. It

It is traditional to break the fast with water and a few dates, the sort of food that the prophet Muhammed would have eaten, rather than eating a big meal immediately. Many people gather in mosques, where dates are served after the sunset prayers, followed by a meal for those who wish to stay. Of course many sweets are also eaten, and the bakeries are extremely busy.

Muslim children praying at the Grand Mosque during the night of al-Qadr, which falls within the last 10 days of the month of Ramadan.

In Kuwait maybe more than in many other Muslim countries, the women go out after the evening meal to meet in special rooms attached to mosques or to visit each other, often with the children dressed in their best clothes. There is an additional treat for children in Kuwait during Ramadan. On the 13th night of the fast, children visit from house to house, singing to the youngest member of each household and collecting gifts and sweets.

also means not smoking, possibly the hardest part for most Kuwaiti men. If the month falls in winter, it is a great relief, as the day is short and the feeling of thirst is not so acute. When the month occurs in the scorchingly hot summer, however, the fast is harder to endure. Many Kuwaitis sleep a great deal during the day at this time and spend their nights eating and socializing, with many offices and businesses closing or slowing down.

THE RAMADAN ROUTINE

For Muslims prayer and fasting during Ramadan give a sense of achievement and closeness to the rest of the Muslim world. Children, women who are pregnant or with small babies, the elderly, and the sick are not expected to fast. Those forced to travel are also excused, although they are expected to make up for the days missed on another occasion. Many people feel fasting is good for the health and teaches self-discipline as well as enhances sensitivity to the suffering of the poor.

A day during the month of Ramadan begins before dawn, often in the middle of the night, when a large meal is eaten before sunrise to prepare for the fast ahead. Restaurants are closed, except those that serve only non-Muslims and travelers, such as the airport coffee shops. The family gathers again at sunset, after prayers, and breaks the fast together. Many traditional dishes are served for this meal, which can last until late in the night. The evenings are occasions for much merriment, followed by visits to relatives and friends, or trips to shops, restaurants, and parks, which stay open late during the month. The whole family often stays awake all night, only going to bed after eating the early breakfast. No wonder children look forward to the fasting month.

THE FESTIVAL OF THE SACRIFICE

The biggest festival in Kuwait is that of Eid al-Adha, or the Festival of the Sacrifice. This commemorates the story of Abraham, who was willing to sacrifice his son on God's orders, a story from the Old Testament familiar to Christians and Jews. God was pleased with Abraham, so he asked him instead to sacrifice a lamb. This festival coincides with the end of the major pilgrimage to Mecca, and all Muslims who can afford it sacrifice a goat or a sheep, eat some of the meat, and share the rest with the poor. Many special meat dishes are eaten so that all the family can share in the sacrifice. Sacrificing an animal, as well as eating it, is important, but the most vital aspect is charity. Many Kuwaitis offer a whole live animal to their servants so that they can have the prestige of offering their own sacrifice. The bedouin bring their sheep and goats to the city to sell at this time, as they will receive the best prices. This festival was traditionally the best opportunity for the bedouin to earn money.

Kuwaiti Muslms at prayer on the first day of Eid al-Adha.

FOOD

A Kuwaiti woman selecting produce from a stall in a market.

CHAPTER 13

M OST ENTERTAINMENT IN KUWAIT revolves around eating. Hospitality is a vital part of both the old bedouin code and the life of modern Kuwaitis. Food and hospitality are inseparable for most Muslims and Arabs, and Kuwaitis are no exception to this rule. Lavish dinners and lunches at home are the most usual form of socializing for families and friends.

The traditional foods in Kuwait were those of the desert bedouin, supplemented by a variety of fish from the Gulf. Trading and, later, oil wealth, enabled Kuwaitis to develop a varied and sophisticated cuisine. Kuwaiti cuisine reflects the long history of trading contacts with other countries and consists of a mixture of Arab, Turkish, Iranian, and Indian food. There is a strong reliance on fish, rice, bread, and fruit. As there are many foreigners, most Kuwaitis are familiar with a great variety of foods. Restaurants offer a varied fare, but as all food should be halal, or deemed suitable by Islamic law, no pork or alcohol is served.

TYPICAL MEALS

Breakfast is usually eaten early, as work and school usually start before 8:00 A.M. It consists of sweet tea or coffee, bread, honey or jam, and dates. Depending on the season, lunch or dinner is the largest meal of the day. Lunch is traditionally followed by an afternoon nap, due to the heat of the afternoon. Dinner is eaten late, when the evening cools

A lot of the food in Kuwait is imported due to the country's unfavorable agricultural conditions. However, this means that a lot of different cuisines can be found in Kuwait. Fish is a commonly featured food in Kuwaiti dishes due to its accessibility. Kuwaitis eat with their right hands because the left one is meant to be used for ablutions.

down. Kuwaitis can stay up late and still rise early in the morning before the worst of the heat, since they take an afternoon nap.

Meals usually start with a variety of appetizers, which are also known as meze, many of which are common to the rest of the Arab world. These may include hummus, a smooth dip made with chickpeas, and tahini, a paste of dried sesame seeds, garlic, salt, paprika, and lemon juice. Other popular appetizers include falafel (deep-fried bean croquettes), *warak al-inab* (stuffed vine leaves), and *samboosa* (pastries filled with meat, vegetables, and cheese).

The main course often consists of fish, sometimes chicken or lamb, and rarely beef. As a food forbidden to Muslims, pork is never served. Fish is an important element in Kuwaiti cooking, and there are many ways of preparing it. Common seafood are *hamour*, similar to sea bass; king prawns; *umm robien*, a type of lobster; and *zabedi*, a whitefish unique to the Gulf. Meat, chicken, and fish are served fried, stewed, stuffed, and barbecued as kebabs. Fish is often served in a curry sauce, as in India.

Tabeekh is a famous cooking method used for preparing many Kuwaiti meals. In this method the entire feast is cooked over heat after being placed in a single container. Another Kuwaiti cooking method is known as *marag*, in which all the important ingredients are fried and prepared before being added to the rest of the meal, which is then cooked over light heat.

Date palms are the most common trees in Kuwait. The dates they produce are an important part of the Kuwaiti diet.

Pizzas, hamburgers, and fried chicken are popular, especially among young people. Fast-food outlets are becoming places for both socializing with friends and family outings. But fast food is unlikely to replace traditional family dining, as Kuwaitis are very attached to dining at home with friends and family. Although Pizza Hut offers pepperoni pizza, there is one difference from the American version: Beef pepperoni, made locally to taste just like the pork version, is used.

Kuwaitis also have their own traditional fast foods, and stalls and small shops in all areas sell kebabs, appetizers, ice cream, and juices. Sandwich bars are also popular and serve both American sandwiches and Arabic foods such as falafel.

For very special occasions, bedouin dishes such as camel meat and whole, stuffed baby lamb cooked in milk are prepared. Rice is a staple of all main courses, often served decorated with almonds and raisins and flavored with meat or fish stock, saffron, and spices.

Desserts are very sweet and not usually served after a meal but as a snack at other times. Common desserts include Turkish baklava, layers of very thin pastry and nuts bathed in a sweet syrup made of sugar and rose water. Almonds, pistachios, walnuts, raisins, cardamoms, rose water, and saffron are common ingredients of desserts.

Fresh fruits may be served after meals, usually chilled and beautifully prepared for the guests. It would be inhospitable to have guests cut up their own fruits. Refreshing fruits such as watermelons are often served after the afternoon nap. Dates are very popular.

MANNERS AND CUSTOMS

Before eating, most Kuwaitis say "*Bismillah,*" which means "in the name of God." Afterward they thank God for such a good meal. In modern Kuwaiti homes food is usually served at dining tables with cutlery and china. Many dining tables can seat 20 or more people. Men and women eat together in cities, unless unrelated male guests are present. For large parties, men and women often eat and entertain separately so that the atmosphere can be

Kuwaiti meals will usually be accompanied by bowls of tomato and garlic sauce (*daqqus*) and yogurt relish (*rob*) to cool the palate after the spicy food.

Coffee is an important symbol of hospitality in Arab countries.

more relaxed. The host always ensures that a guest has plenty to eat and his plate is never empty. It can be difficult for the guest to decline when full without offending the host, who might assume that the guest is unhappy with the food.

BEDOUIN DINING

More traditional people and particularly bedouin may eat sitting on rugs and cushions on the floor, using low tables or a tablecloth spread on the floor. They sit with one leg tucked in beneath them and the other leg with the knee raised so that they can rest their arms on the knee. Men and women eat separately, with the women sometimes eating after the men have finished the choicest morsels. The diners share common serving dishes, from which they eat with their fingers, having previously washed their hands. Only their right hand is used to eat, and only from that part of the dish closest to them. Pieces of large loaves of flat bread, baked on a convex tray placed over a fire, are used to pick up the food and soak up the sauces.

Bedouin food was, by necessity, very simple. Milk and milk products, such as yogurt, remain a major part of the diet, which also includes grains such as wheat, dates, and very little meat. Animals are more useful for their milk than as meat. The only time some bedouin would eat meat was when a sheep or a camel was slaughtered to celebrate a special occasion. Foods such as soups, rice, and seeds are enriched by the addition of clarified butter. To clarify butter, the butter is heated and then cooled; the clear yellow liquid that is strained off the top is the clarified butter, which can be kept in a tin. Fruits and vegetables, other than dates, were rare in the traditional bedouin diet, as it is not possible to grow such things in the desert.

FOOD PREPARATION

Because many Kuwaiti dishes require lengthy preparation, most houses employ foreign servants to help with the cooking, serving, and cleaning up.

HALAL OR *HARAM?*

Muslims are not to eat pork, venison, or any animal that died a natural death. These are haram *(har-AHM), or forbidden. For an animal to be fit for consumption, the person killing it must use a sharp knife while invoking God's blessings (*bismillah*), and it must be drained of its blood. It is then halal, allowed. The products of* haram *animals must be avoided in other food, such as cookies and ice cream. For some Muslims, shellfish such as shrimp are considered* haram. *But this has not traditionally been so in the Gulf countries, where they are part of the diet. Alcohol in any form is forbidden, as is handling it or remaining in a place where it is sold or consumed. In Kuwait, alcohol is banned completely, which is not to say that some Kuwaitis do not drink it secretly at home.*

Many Kuwaiti women will cook much of the food themselves but delegate the arduous preparation to servants. The tastes and styles of the foreign servants have influenced the nature of Kuwaiti cooking greatly, making it spicier and more varied than the food of most other Arab countries.

Many Kuwaiti houses have two kitchens: one inside for preparation, snacks, tea, and coffee, and one outside, which is ideally situated far from the living quarters. This is where lengthy and hot baking and other cooking are done. Much Kuwaiti food has a very strong smell, and the heat generated from cooking is most unwelcome in the hot climate. Kuwaitis try to keep their houses a cool refuge from the scorching streets.

YOU BUY, WE COOK! For people who do not have an outside kitchen, most neighborhoods have small cooking shops. Manned by just one person and owned by immigrants, these kitchens specialize in preparing hot dishes, especially fish, according to the customer's instructions. These shops are now part of all planned housing developments. Once a fish is purchased at the market, it can be taken to this shop, where the spices to be used will be discussed. After about an hour, a phone call from the shop will let the customer know his fish dish is ready for collection.

"The unexpected guest is a gift from God."—saying popularly believed to be the prophet Muhammed's.
"The guest is king."—popular Arab saying. These two sayings form the basic principle of Kuwaiti social life.

ARABIC HONEY CAKE

3 eggs

½ cup (125 ml) granulated
  white sugar

½ teaspoon (2.5 ml) vanilla extract

⅓ cup (85 ml) butter, melted

½ cup (125 ml) plus 1 tablespoon
  (15 ml) all-purpose flour

½ teaspoon (2.5 ml) baking powder

Topping

½ cup (125 ml) butter

½ cup (125 ml) granulated
  white sugar

⅓ cup (85 ml) honey

½ cup (125 ml) slivered almonds

½ teaspoon (2.5 ml) ground
  cinnamon

Grease a 10-inch cake pan. Preheat the oven to 400°F (205°C). Beat the eggs, sugar, and vanilla extract until the mixture whitens. Add the melted butter and mix well. Sift the flour and the baking powder together, and gently stir in to the existing mixture. Pour the batter into the prepared pan, and bake for 10—12 minutes. Meanwhile prepare the topping. Melt the butter on medium heat. Add the rest of the ingredients, and bring to a boil, stirring constantly. Pour the topping gently onto the cake, and return it to the oven for another 15—20 minutes.

MACHBOUS RUBYAN (RICE WITH SHRIMP)

2 cups (500 ml) basmati rice

2 large onions, chopped

6 cloves garlic, chopped

4 tablespoons (60 ml) ghee
(clarified butter)

2.2 pounds (1 kg) shrimp, shelled

2 teaspoons (10 ml) curry powder

2 cinnamon sticks

2 bay leaves

1 teaspoon (5 ml) cardamom, ground

4 tomatoes, peeled and chopped

¼ cup (60 ml) coriander leaves, chopped

A pinch of salt

¼ teaspoon (1 ml) black pepper, ground

1 teaspoon (5 ml) turmeric

1 ½ (375 ml) cups water

½ cup (125 ml) almonds

Soak rice. Fry onions and garlic in ghee in a large pan until golden brown. Add shrimp, curry powder, cinnamon, bay leaves, and cardamom. Cook until the shrimp become opaque in color. Remove half of the shrimp and keep aside. To the pan add tomatoes, coriander, salt, pepper and turmeric. Stir over heat for 5 minutes. Add water. Bring to a boil, and then simmer for 3—5 minutes. Drain rice, and stir into sauce. Bring to a boil, and simmer for 10 minutes. Cover tightly, and simmer over low heat for another 25—30 minutes or until rice is cooked. Boil almonds. Remove their shells, and halve. Fry until golden brown. Serve the rice on a large platter. Add reserved shrimp and fried almonds to garnish.

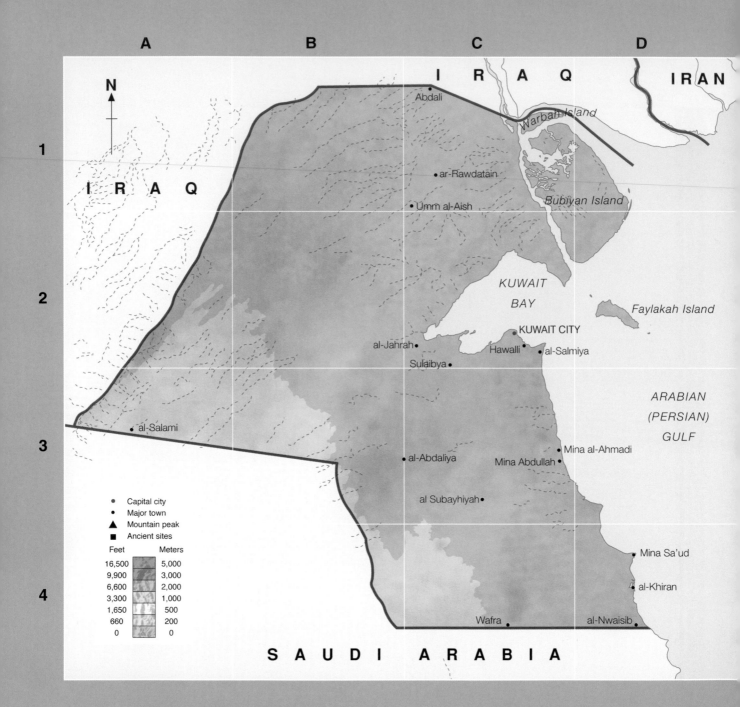

N

A   B   C   D

I R A Q   **I R A N**

Abdali

Warbah Island

1

I R A Q

• ar-Rawdatain

Bubiyan Island

• Umm al-Aish

KUWAIT

BAY

2

Faylakah Island

KUWAIT CITY

al-Jahrah •   Hawalli •   • al-Salmiya

Sulaibya •

ARABIAN

(PERSIAN)

• al-Salami   *GULF*

3

• al-Abdaliya   Mina al-Ahmadi •

Mina Abdullah •

• Capital city

• Major town   al Subayhiyah •

▲ Mountain peak

■ Ancient sites

Mina Sa'ud •

Feet	Meters
16,500	5,000
9,900	3,000
6,600	2,000
3,300	1,000
1,650	500
660	200
0	0

• al-Khiran

4

Wafra •   al-Nwaisib •

S A U D I   A R A B I A

MAP OF KUWAIT

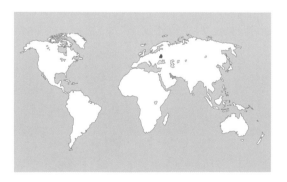

ECONOMIC KUWAIT

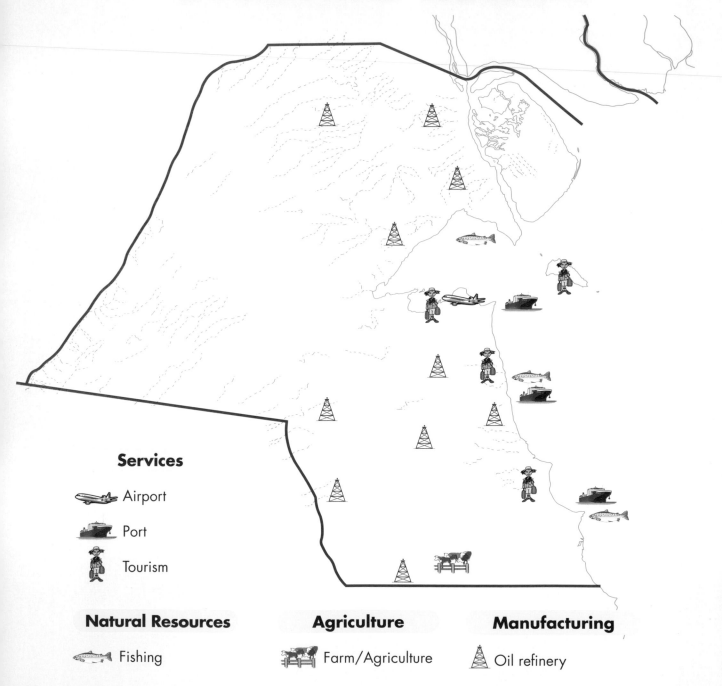

Services

✈ Airport

🚢 Port

🧍 Tourism

Natural Resources

🐟 Fishing

Agriculture

🐄 Farm/Agriculture

Manufacturing

⛏ Oil refinery

ABOUT THE ECONOMY

OVERVIEW

Kuwait has a small, wealthy, open economy with crude oil reserves of about 101.5 billion barrels—estimated to be 8 percent of the world reserves. Petroleum makes up nearly half of the income of the country, most of its export revenues, and 5 percent of government income. High oil prices in recent years have helped make Kuwait a very wealthy country, with huge savings controlled by the government. Kuwait lacks water and has almost no farmland. Apart from fish, the country depends almost wholly on imports for food and water.

GROSS DOMESTIC PRODUCT (GDP)

$111.3 billion (2007 estimates)

GDP PER CAPITA

$24,040 (2006)

GROWTH RATE

4.6 percent (2007 estimates)

LABOR FORCE

2.093 million; non-Kuwaitis represent about 80 percent of the labor force (2007 estimates)

CURRENCY

Kuwait Dinar (KD)
USD1 = 0.287 Kuwaiti dinar (KD) (2009)

MAIN EXPORTS

Oil and refined products, fertilizers

MAIN IMPORTS

Food, construction materials, vehicles and parts, clothing

MAIN TRADE PARTNERS

United States, Japan, South Korea, Taiwan, Singapore, the Netherlands, China

AGRICULTURAL PRODUCTS

Fish

INDUSTRIES

Petroleum, petrochemicals, cement, shipbuilding and repair, water desalination, food processing, construction materials

OIL PRODUCTION

2.669 million barrels per day (2005 estimates)

OIL RESERVES

101.5 billion barrels (2007 estimates)

NATURAL RESOURCES

Petroleum, fish, shrimp, natural gas

CULTURAL KUWAIT

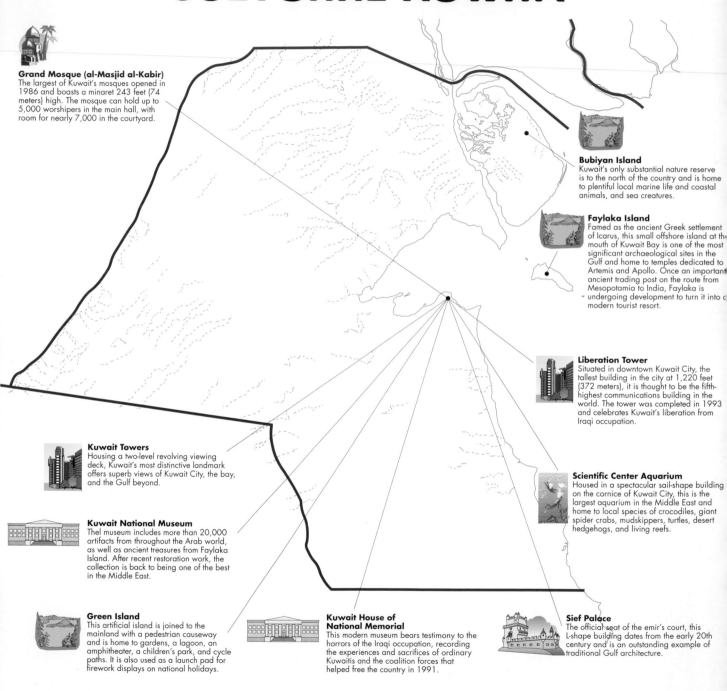

Grand Mosque (al-Masjid al-Kabir)
The largest of Kuwait's mosques opened in 1986 and boasts a minaret 243 feet (74 meters) high. The mosque can hold up to 5,000 worshipers in the main hall, with room for nearly 7,000 in the courtyard.

Bubiyan Island
Kuwait's only substantial nature reserve is to the north of the country and is home to plentiful local marine life and coastal animals, and sea creatures.

Faylaka Island
Famed as the ancient Greek settlement of Icarus, this small offshore island at the mouth of Kuwait Bay is one of the most significant archaeological sites in the Gulf and home to temples dedicated to Artemis and Apollo. Once an important ancient trading post on the route from Mesopotamia to India, Faylaka is undergoing development to turn it into a modern tourist resort.

Liberation Tower
Situated in downtown Kuwait City, the tallest building in the city at 1,220 feet (372 meters), it is thought to be the fifth-highest communications building in the world. The tower was completed in 1993 and celebrates Kuwait's liberation from Iraqi occupation.

Kuwait Towers
Housing a two-level revolving viewing deck, Kuwait's most distinctive landmark offers superb views of Kuwait City, the bay, and the Gulf beyond.

Scientific Center Aquarium
Housed in a spectacular sail-shape building on the cornice of Kuwait City, this is the largest aquarium in the Middle East and home to local species of crocodiles, giant spider crabs, mudskippers, turtles, desert hedgehogs, and living reefs.

Kuwait National Museum
Thel museum includes more than 20,000 artifacts from throughout the Arab world, as well as ancient treasures from Faylaka Island. After recent restoration work, the collection is back to being one of the best in the Middle East.

Green Island
This artificial island is joined to the mainland with a pedestrian causeway and is home to gardens, a lagoon, an amphitheater, a children's park, and cycle paths. It is also used as a launch pad for firework displays on national holidays.

Kuwait House of National Memorial
This modern museum bears testimony to the horrors of the Iraqi occupation, recording the experiences and sacrifices of ordinary Kuwaitis and the coalition forces that helped free the country in 1991.

Sief Palace
The official seat of the emir's court, this L-shape building dates from the early 20th century and is an outstanding example of traditional Gulf architecture.

ABOUT THE CULTURE

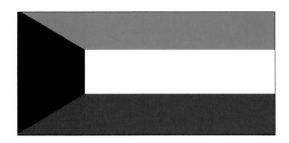

OFFICIAL NAME
Dawlat al-Kuwayt (State of Kuwait)

NATIONAL FLAG
Three equal horizontal bands of green (top), white, and red with a black trapezoid on the hoist side; the design, which dates to 1961, is based on the Arab revolt flag of World War I.

NATIONALITY
Kuwaiti

CAPITAL
Kuwait City

LAND AREA
6,880 square miles (17,820 square km)

POPULATION
2,596,799, including 1.3 million nonnationals (2008 estimates)

ADMINISTRATIVE AREAS
Six governorates: al-Ahmadi, al-Asimah, al-Farwaniyah, al-Jahra, Hawalli, Mubarak al-Kabir

OFFICIAL LANGUAGE
Arabic (English is also widely spoken)

ETHNIC GROUPS
Kuwaiti 45 percent, other Arab 35 percent, South Asian 9 percent, Iranian 4 percent, other 7 percent

MAJOR RELIGIONS
Muslim 85 percent (Sunni 70 percent, Shiites 30 percent), other (includes Christian, Hindu, Parsi) 15 percent

HOLIDAYS AND FESTIVALS
National Day, February 25
Liberation Day, February 26

BIRTHRATE
21.9 births per 1,000 population (2008 estimates)

DEATH RATE
2.37 deaths per 1,000 population (2008 estimates)

FERTILITY RATE
2.81 children born per woman (2008 estimates)

LIFE EXPECTANCY
Total: 77.53 years
Male: 76.38 years
Female: 78.73 years (2008 estimates)

TIME LINE

IN KUWAIT	IN THE WORLD
	323 B.C. Alexander the Great's empire stretches from Greece to India.
	1206–1368 Genghis Khan unifies the Mongols and starts conquest of the world. At its height, the Mongol Empire under Kublai Khan stretches from China to Persia and parts of Europe and Russia.
1700s Settlers arrive at the site of the present-day Kuwait City from the interior of the Arabian Peninsula.	
1756 Kuwait comes under the control of the al-Sabah family, ancestors of Kuwait's current rulers.	
	1789–99 The French Revolution
1899 Sheikh Mubarak al-Sabah strikes a deal with Britain, and Kuwait becomes a British protectorate.	
	1914 World War I begins.
1937 Large oil reserves are discovered by the U.S.-British Kuwait Oil Company.	
	1939 World War II begins.
	1945 The United States drops atomic bombs on Hiroshima and Nagasaki.
1961 Kuwait becomes independent and joins the Arab League. Iraq renews claims that Kuwait is part of its territory but backs down after British military threats.	
1963 Elections held for National Assembly under terms of the newly drafted constitution.	
1976 The emir suspends the National Assembly.	
1980 Iran-Iraq War: Kuwait supports Iraq, giving its larger neighbor money to conduct the war.	

IN KUWAIT	IN THE WORLD
1981 • The National Assembly is recalled. **1990** • Iraq invades and then annexes Kuwait over an oil dispute. The emir and cabinet flee to Saudi Arabia. **1991** • Iraq fails to comply with a UN resolution ordering it to withdraw. A U.S.-led and UN-backed aerial bombing campaign begins in Kuwait and Iraq in January. **1993** • The UN draws a new Kuwait-Iraq border, giving a port and a number of oil wells to Kuwait. **1994** • Iraq officially recognizes Kuwait's independence and the UN-demarcated borders. **2003** •• Tens of thousands of soldiers converge on the Kuwait-Iraq border for a U.S.-led military campaign to disarm and oust Iraqi leader Saddam Hussein. Sheikh Sabah al-Ahmad al-Sabah is appointed prime minister. **2005** • Women gain the right to vote and run for office. The first woman cabinet minister, Massouma al-Mubarak, is appointed. **2006** • The emir, Sheikh Jaber III al-Ahmad al-Jaber al-Sabah, dies. Sheikh Sabah IV al-Ahmad al-Sabah is sworn in as emir. Women cast their votes for the first time, in a municipal by-election. **2007**• Sheikh Nasir Muhammad al-Ahmad al-Sabah is appointed prime minister.	• **1986** Nuclear power disaster at Chernobyl in Ukraine. • **1997** Hong Kong is returned to China. • **2003** War in Iraq begins.

GLOSSARY

abaya
A black cloak worn by women that covers the head and clothes

bidoon (be-DOON)
Person denied Kuwaiti citizenship for lack of proof that his or her parents or grandparents were born in Kuwait

burka
A mask that covers the face and body, worn by women

bushiya (boosh-ee-YAH)
A black cloth covering the face

dhow
Traditional Kuwaiti wooden boat

dishdasha
Long robe worn by Kuwaiti men

diwaniyah (dee-WAHN-ee-yah)
A social gathering, usually for men, where business and politics are discussed

gatra (GAT-rah)
Scarf worn by men to cover their heads

hajj
The pilgrimage to Mecca prescribed of Muslims at least once in a lifetime

halal
Food that Muslims are permitted to consume

haram (har-AHM)
Food forbidden to Muslims

hijab
Islamic hair or head covering for women

oud
Arab stringed instrument similar to a guitar

Ramadan
The month of fasting and extra prayer for Muslims

sadu (sa-DOO)
Traditional bedouin weaving

salat (sal-AT)
Muslim requirement of praying five times a day in a prescribed manner

saum (sowm)
Fasting between sunrise and sunset during month of Ramadan

Sayyed
A descendant of the prophet Muhammed

shahada (sha-ha-DAH)
Professing faith

sirwal (seer-WAHL)
Long white trousers worn by men

Sunni
The branch of Islam to which the majority of Muslims belong

thob (thohb)
A long, loose dress

zakat (za-KAAT)
Giving alms to the needy or to good causes

FOR FURTHER INFORMATION

BOOKS

Dipiazza, Francesca Davis. *Kuwait in Pictures* (Visual Geography. Second Series). Minneapolis: Twenty-First Century Books, 2006.

Gay, Kathlyn and Martin Gay. *Persian Gulf War* (Voices from the Past.). New York: Twenty-First Century Books, 1997.

Holden, Henry M. *The Persian Gulf War* (U.S. Wars). Berkeley Heights, NJ: Enslow Publishers, 2003.

Isiorho, Soloman A., and Gritzner, Charles. *Kuwait* (Modern World Nations). New York: Chelsea House Publishers, 2004.

Marcovitz, Hal. *Kuwait* (Modern Middle East Nations and Their Strategic Place in the World). Broomall, PA: Mason Crest Publishers, 2003.

Miller, Debra A. *Kuwait* (Modern Nations of the World). San Diego, CA: Lucent Books, 2004.

Walker, Jenny. *Oman, UAE, and the Arabian Peninsula* (Lonely Planet Multi Country Guide). London: Lonely Planet Publications, 2007.

Willis, Terri. *Kuwait* (Enchantment of the World, Second Series). Danbury, CT: Children's Press, 2007.

Zwier, Lawrence J., and Matthew Scott Weltig. *The Persian Gulf and Iraqi Wars* (Chronicle of America's Wars). Minneapolis: Lerner Publishing Group, 2004.

MUSIC

Ensemble Al-Umayri. *The Sawt in Kuwait*. Navras, 2003.

Various artists. *Music from the Arabian Gulf*. Arc Music, 2007.

Various artists. *Persian Gulf Expressway*. Naqmeh Banafsh Andisheh Cultural Institute, 2007.

FILMS

History Channel Presents: Operation Desert Storm. A&E Television Networks.

BIBLIOGRAPHY

Casey, Michael S. *The History of Kuwait* (The Greenwood Histories of the Modern Nations). Westport, CT: Greenwood Press, 2007.

Crystal, Jill. *Oil and Politics in the Gulf: Rulers and Merchants in Kuwait and Qatar*. Cambridge, England: Cambridge University Press, 1995.

Mallos, Tess. *Cooking of the Gulf: Bahrain, Kuwait, Oman, Qatar, Saudi Arabia, United Arab Emirates*. Boone, NC: Parkway Publishing, 2004.

Robinson, Gordon and Paul Greenway. *Bahrain, Kuwait, and Qatar* (Lonely Planet Regional Guides). London: Lonely Planet Publications, 2000.

Slot, Ben J. and William Facey. *Mubarak Al-Sabah: Founder of Modern Kuwait, 1896—1915*. London: Arabian Publishing, 2005.

Smith, Simon. *Kuwait, 1950—1965: Britain, the Al-Sabah, and Oil*. Oxford, England: Oxford University Press, 2000.

Tetreault, M. A. *Stories of Democracy: Politics and Society in Contemporary Kuwait*. New York: Columbia University Press, 2000.

Villiers, Alan et al. *Sons of Sindbad: Sailing with the Arabs in Their Dhows, in the Red Sea, Round the Coasts of Arabia, and to Zanzibar and Tanganyika, Pearling in the Persian... the Shipmasters and the Mariners of Kuwait*. London: Arabian Publishing, 2006.

WEBSITES

Charts & Numbers. www.chartsandnumbers.com

Kuwait Info. www.kuwait-info.com

Kuwait Petroleum Corporation. www.kpc.com.kw

Kuwait Pocket Guide. www.kuwaitpocketguide.com

Kuwait Times. www.kuwaittimes.net

Kuwait Today. www.kuwaittoday.com

Kuwaitiah.net. www.kuwaitiah.net

INDEX

INDEX